Puffin Books

The Green Piper

After a sudden, mysterious flash of light in the night sky over their town, Angie, Ross and their friend Mad Jack are affected by a strange haunting music drifting from the woodland nearby. It's weird – what happens to the place after that. Alone, unaided, they investigate. And what they discover is both bewildering and sinister . . .

This is another gripping novel from one of Australia's most outstanding authors: Victor Kelleher was born in London and as a teenager travelled to Africa where he lived for twenty years. His first book for young people was *Forbidden Paths of Thual*. Since then he has written *The Hunting of Shadroth, Master of the Grove* (Australian Children's Book of the Year, 1983), *Papio* (shortlisted for the Australian Children's Book of the Year, 1985), *Taronga* (named an Honour Book at the Australian Children's Book of the Year Awards, 1987), *The Makers* (shortlisted for the 1988 Awards), *Baily's Bones, The Red King* (shortlisted for the 1990 Awards) and *Brother Night* (an Honour Book in 1991). Victor now lives in Sydney and is a full-time writer.

Also by Victor Kelleher

Forbidden Paths of Thual

The Hunting of Shadroth

Master of the Grove

Papio

Taronga

The Makers

Baily's Bones

The Red King

Brother Night

THE GREEN PIPER

VICTOR KELLEHER

PUFFIN BOOKS

Puffin Books
Penguin Books Australia Ltd
487 Maroondah Highway, PO Box 257
Ringwood, Victoria, 3134, Australia
Penguin Books Ltd
Harmondsworth, Middlesex, England
Viking Penguin, A Division of Penguin Books USA Inc.
375 Hudson Street, New York, New York 10014, USA
Penguin Books Canada Limited
10 Alcorn Avenue, Toronto, Ontario, Canada M4V 1E4
Penguin Books (N.Z.) Ltd
182-190 Wairau Road, Auckland 10, New Zealand

First published 1984 by Viking Kestrel
Published in Puffin, 1987
This edition published 1991
10 9 8 7 6 5

Typeset in Plantin by Dudley E. King
Offset from the Viking Kestrel edition
Printed and bound in Australia by The Book Printer, Victoria

National Library of Australia
Cataloguing-in-Publication data:

Kelleher, Victor, 1939-
The green piper.
ISBN 0 14 032251 5.
I. Title.
A823.3

CONTENTS

AUTHOR'S ACKNOWLEDGEMENT

I wish to thank the Literature Board of the Australia Council whose kind assistance enabled me to write this book.

PART I
SPRING

ONE

None of them actually saw it, so they could not say later, yes, that was definitely the beginning, that was how the whole thing started. It was no more definite than a flash or faint sparkle, something half glimpsed rather than actually seen. A brief suggestion of light and movement, gone before it could be brought into focus – leaving the spring evening, the waning dusk, apparently unchanged.

Or very nearly so.

From the tall trees bordering the village, a colony of rooks rose, cawing, into the deepening twilight. While in the village a number of dogs barked uneasily, as at a full moon.

'What was that?' Bill Miller asked.

He had been digging in his cottage garden, but now he straightened up and rested on his spade, gazing quizzically at the darkening sky and then across to his son, Ross, who was lounging on the kitchen step.

'I'm not sure,' Ross said. 'Maybe some kid's rocket.'

'Bit quick for a rocket, wasn't it? And look at the rabbits.'

Like the rooks, they were showing signs of agitation, hopping nervously about their wooden hutch, one large buck clawing at the wire mesh.

Ross went over to them, poked a finger through the mesh and gently rubbed the buck's nose. 'Settle down now,' he said soothingly.

From where he was standing he had a clear view over the fence into the next-door garden. Angie, a girl of his own age, was crouched on the concrete path, her back to him. She and her family had moved into the neighbouring cottage only a few weeks earlier, so he hardly knew her. He cleared his throat, trying to attract her attention.

'Any idea what that might have been?' he asked.

She glanced over her shoulder, leaning back slightly, and he saw past her, to where a cat was standing with its back arched, its fur on end. 'No, I'm sorry, I was looking at the cat.'

'D'you know what scared it?'

She shook her head and again turned her attention to the frightened animal, lightly stroking its fur with the back of her fingers. As Ross watched her, the shrill voice of Mrs Bowles, Angie's mother, came floating through the open window of the cottage: 'George, what's going on out there?'

George Bowles popped his round, balding head out of an upstairs window and grinned at Angie. 'Hard to say, my dear,' he answered in a much milder tone. 'Probably one of those UFO things' – laughing good naturedly at his own suggestion.

Bill Miller, meanwhile, was still resting on his spade. 'Could have been one of those weather balloon things, I suppose,' he muttered. 'I've seen about them on telly. How they can shine bright as day if they're high enough. Sort of wink at you, then gone.'

He was about to resume his digging when there was a pounding of feet in the lane and Nigel, who lived at the far end of the row of cottages, thrust his thin, pinched face over the back fence. His round spectacles, reflecting the light from the kitchen window, shone like pale yellow moons.

'Did you see it?' he burst out in a high squeaky voice.

'Here we go,' Ross murmured disgustedly, 'old eagle eye strikes again.'

'But I did! I saw it!'

'Trust you.'

'Honest, Ross. A comet. Tail and all.'

'For pity's sake! It was only there for a split second. And you wouldn't know a comet from a firefly.'

'Interesting idea, that,' Bill Miller said thoughtfully, fingering his braces which hung down over his thighs in loops. 'A comet. Pretty fast, aren't they?'

'Yes,' Angie said, 'but I think they're visible for a while.' She had moved closer to the fence, the cat cradled in her arms.

'There you are, then,' Ross said.

'What does a girl know about it?' Nigel protested.

Ross turned apologetically towards Angie. 'Don't take any notice of the shrimp. He has a habit of coming out with remarks like that.'

She shrugged indifferently. 'Why don't you ask Mad Jack?' she suggested. 'He's always gazing at the sky.'

Further down the lane someone was singing 'Three Blind Mice' in a high quavery voice. A few moments later an old man shuffled into view. He was wearing a crumpled trilby hat and a long overcoat that reached almost to his heels.

'Evening, Jack,' Ross called out.

The old man raised his hat in greeting, revealing a bald head fringed with wispy grey hair.

'Daft old coot,' Bill Miller muttered, turning over a spadeful of earth.

'Aye, daft,' he agreed with a chuckle, shaking his head vigorously. 'Daft old Jack, that's me.'

'But sharp too, when you want to be,' Ross added quickly, smiling at him. 'Isn't that so, Jack?'

'Aye, sharp enough. Sharp as a . . . as an axe.'

'Tell us then, Jack. What did you see tonight?'

'See?' – his hat still raised, his head nodding slowly.

'Yes. Up there. A few minutes back.'

From the darkening sky came a series of loud caws; and the cat, lying quietly in Angie's arms, suddenly raked its claws across the back of her hand and leaped off into the shadows.

'What . . . ?' Angie began, startled.

But Jack, placing his hat back on his head, had already started singing in his high quavery voice:

Twinkle, twinkle, little star,
How I wonder what you are.

TWO

Ross cleared the dishes from the table and carried them through to the kitchen. His father, still in his work clothes, was standing at the window looking out at the back garden.

'I can't understand it,' he said. 'I only dug that patch over last week and it's already smothered in weeds.'

'It is spring,' Ross reminded him, running hot water into the sink.

'Maybe. But I've never known a spring like this one. The grass, too, growing like mad. Even pushing up through the asphalt at the end of the lane.'

'Through the asphalt? Come on, Dad, pull the other one.'

'I'm telling you. Along the edges where it's thin. Lifting it like a bit of dried clay.'

Ross peered past his father's broad shoulders at the narrow strip of garden. He had to admit, it was unusually overgrown. As was the field beyond the lane, the grass already knee-deep and lush, the way it sometimes grew in a particularly damp summer. The distant trees were equally well advanced for the time of year, their branches weighed down with thick clusters of young foliage.

'A good season for the farmers, anyway,' he remarked.

'Yes,' his father agreed, grinning meaningfully at him, 'but not so good for anyone who has to mow the front lawn.'

He gave his son a friendly shove and wandered through to the living room. Ross, busy with the washing up, heard him switch on the television and slump down in a nearby chair. But instead of the news which normally came on at that time, the house was suddenly filled with the deafening roar of static interference.

'What the hell . . .!' his father exclaimed, frantically twiddling the nobs on the old black-and-white set.

Ross, his hands still wet, ran to the living-room door. 'What's up?' he shouted.

'This damn thing! Must be the tube going!'

There was a thump on the intervening wall and the sound of Mrs Bowles' voice raised in protest.

'All right! All right!' his father yelled back. He switched the set off angrily. 'More trouble than it's worth,' he grumbled, settling back with the evening paper. 'Better off without it.'

Ross made no reply, for in the abrupt silence he was aware of something else: a feeling in the air around him; a kind of vibration unlinked to any identifiable sound. He thought at first it was nothing more than ringing in his ears, from the deafening noise of the television. But when he returned to the kitchen, it persisted – except that now it was unmistakably separate from himself, as though the atmosphere in or about the house had developed a life of its own, a steady background hum which existed just beyond the range of hearing.

'Can you feel that?' he called out.

But his father was already asleep, lying back in the armchair, the open newspaper fallen across his face.

Leaving the drying up, Ross wiped his hands and stepped out into the garden. There the odd sensation was stronger still, as much a part of the evening as the dusty slivers of sunlight which filtered through the gaps between the distant trees. It seemed to pulse slightly, coming and going in a regular wave motion.

'What do you think it is then, lad?'

He turned and saw the round, rather high-coloured face of Mr Bowles staring at him across the fence.

8

'Haven't a clue,' he answered truthfully.

'It's peculiar all right. The wife thought it was your telly. Sent me to complain.'

'Yes, sorry about the noise. We couldn't help it.'

'That's all right, lad. The minute I came out here I knew this was something different. More like ... like electricity that's leaked into the air. Is that possible d'you think?'

'I suppose a short circuit's a kind of leak. Whether it could escape into the air though ... '

'Or maybe one of those electrical storms. There is a bit of cloud around.'

Yet as they could both see, it was the wrong sort of cloud: too soft and fluffy, touched with pink by the setting sun.

'Ah well, I expect it'll sort itself out,' Mr Bowles murmured resignedly and disappeared back into the cottage.

Left to himself, Ross stood for a minute or two on the back step, watching and listening. There was, he soon realized, something else peculiar about the evening: a general air of restlessness. Birds flying rapidly overhead, all moving towards the trees at the far edge of the field; something small and furtive padding quietly along the lane; the tall grass in the field shaken by tiny creatures scurrying through it; and from somewhere close at hand, a frantic scratching and a creak of wood.

He looked at the rabbit hutch, half smothered by the recent growth of grass, and saw that the mesh door was bulging outwards, the four rabbits scrabbling at the wire.

'Steady on,' he said quietly.

But before he could reach them, their combined weight bent back the flimsy wooden catch and they came tumbling out. He groped for one, missed, and scrambled to his feet, running to shut the back gate. They were close behind him and he spread his arms wide, expecting them to turn aside, but they kept coming, their movements precise and well regulated, more like mechanical toys than live animals.

'Shoo!' he cried out, 'shoo!'

To no effect. He might as well have been invisible. Ignoring his presence, the biggest of the females leaped beneath his outstretched arm, balanced momentarily on the top of the fence, and dropped into the lane. The buck tried the same manoeuvre and Ross caught it in mid-air, only to discover that he was clinging to a bundle of fury. Letting out a shrill cry, it lunged with its powerful hind legs, scoring his wrist and forearm. He clutched it by the ears and held it at arm's length, but it continued to struggle, its whole body closing up and then catapulting open with such force that it tore itself free. In a second it was up and over the fence in pursuit of the females.

Bewildered by their behaviour, Ross yanked open the gate and hurried after them. They were hopping vigorously down the lane towards a point where it opened into the field. Nor were they alone. The squat figure of a badger was lumbering on ahead of them; and bringing up the rear, its thin legs darting to and fro, was a hedgehog.

Ross paused, nonplussed, and immediately detected the strong, musty odour of a fox. He glanced around just as a big dog fox came galloping past. It too seemed unaware of him, its brush held low, its eyes fixed on something ahead. He thought then that he understood what was happening – why the rabbits had panicked and struggled to escape. Yet to his surprise the fox ignored the rabbits, simply veering around them.

It was not far now from the entrance to the field. A few more strides would have carried it through the opening and into the long grass. But as the fox swung to the left, something happened. It seemed to fold at the knees and slither chin first onto the ground, its body slack and unresisting. The other animals were also collapsing – and almost simultaneously small feathery shapes came tumbling from the sky. There was a soft thud, followed by a heavier impact near by – and lying almost at Ross's feet was a sparrow, its twig-like legs pointing straight up, its wings half open. He touched it gently with one finger and saw from the brightness of its eyes that it was still alive, watching him, yet unable to move. A barn owl, lying close by, had not been so fortunate, the impact having broken its neck.

Ross looked up at the sky. There was not a bird in sight, the cottage gardens unnaturally silent.

Leaving the two bodies where they had fallen, he walked to where the animals were sprawled out on the ground. Like the sparrow, they were still alive, their eyes bright and watchful, their bodies strangely unresponsive. He crouched beside the fox whose tongue was hanging limply from its mouth. Its reddish-brown eyes flicked up towards his face and past him.

'What's the matter, boy?' he murmured.

Angie, approaching silently from behind, crouched beside him. 'It looks like some kind of fit,' she said.

'Yes, but why should they all be affected?'

'I don't know. Perhaps it has something to do with the field. That's where they were heading.'

'You saw what happened, then?'

She nodded. 'I was watching from the upstairs window. There was a bang on the roof and then everything was falling over. It was as if someone had turned off a switch.'

'Yes, it was a bit like a ... '

He broke off as the fox snarled and scrambled to its feet, bounding back down the lane. The other animals were also staggering up: the badger blinking sleepily in the evening light; the rabbits crowding into the partial shelter of the fence.

'Let's round them up while we've got the chance,' Angie said.

'Just a minute.' Ross's face was raised as though he were listening. 'Do you notice anything different?'

'Different?'

'That tingling feeling in the air – it's gone.'

She turned her head slowly from side to side. 'Yes, it has.'

'And just now you mentioned ...'

But at that moment Nigel came running down the lane. 'Hey,

Ross!' he called excitedly. 'Did you see old Jones's pigeons? One
minute they were flying, and the next . . .'

THREE

'We could have a quick look round,' Ross suggested.

'I'd rather not,' Angie said.

'But why?'

They were standing at the opening to Elm Walk, facing each other. The great trees which gave their name to the street had recently died from disease and now stood gaunt and bare against the cloudy sky. At the far end of the Walk some council workmen were attaching ropes to the first of the trees in preparation for taking it down.

'After all,' Ross went on, 'you were the one who noticed how everything was heading for the field.'

'That doesn't mean I . . .'

The rest of what she said was drowned out by the snarl of a chainsaw and the crash of falling wood.

'What did you say?' Ross asked.

'It doesn't matter.'

'But it does. Birds can't drop from the sky for no reason. If we don't find out why, someone else soon will.'

'I don't think so. I mentioned it to some of the kids at school and they didn't know what I was talking about.'

'All right. But what about other people along the lane? They must have seen something.'

She kicked at the thick stems of grass thrusting up through

13

the cracks in the pavement. Near to where she was standing one of the curbstones had been slightly dislodged by a vigorous clump of dandelions.

'Dad reckons it was some kind of electrical interference,' she answered slowly. 'He says it could have confused the birds as well as affecting your telly.'

'Is that what you believe?'

She hesitated as the chainsaw snarled again and another limb came tumbling down. 'No, there's probably more to it than that.'

'So what harm is there in having a look round?'

'I've told you – I don't want to.'

Someone had started shouting at the workmen in a shrill voice, and Ross stared gloomily down the Walk.

'It's because of your mum, isn't it?' he said at last. 'She doesn't want you mixing with people like me.'

'She does talk like that sometimes,' Angie admitted, 'but ...'

'I suppose she's been gossiping with old Hughes in the corner shop,' he broke in bitterly. 'Thinks I'll be a bad influence or something.'

'If you'd let me finish,' she said tersely, 'I was about to say I don't agree with her – and neither does Dad. She's not my reason for refusing.'

'Then what is?'

'It's hard to explain. I just find the whole thing spooky. Sort of unnatural.'

'That's exactly why I want to have a look.'

'Well I'm not stopping you.'

Slightly disgruntled with each other, they made their way along the Walk. At the far end, the argument which had broken out a minute or two earlier was now in full swing, with a middle-aged woman shouting at the group of rather surprised workmen.

'Vandals!' she was saying. 'That's what you are. Vandals!

Grown men, who should know better. Acting like bar-barians!'

The foreman, partly amused and partly angered by her, took a piece of crumpled white paper from his pocket. 'You'd better check our work sheet before you start calling us names,' he said. 'See for yourself. It says here we're to take down the dead trees in Elm Walk.'

'But that's just it: they aren't dead! Look at them!' She pointed to tiny green shoots sprouting from the main branches. 'Is that what you expect to find on a dead tree?'

'It says here . . .' the foreman repeated doggedly.

'I don't care what it says! The trees are still alive!'

She turned imploringly to Ross.'You, young man, surely you can make them see sense.'

But Ross had recognized his father amongst the workmen. Bill Miller winked at him and jerked his head, indicating that he should continue on home.

' . . . er . . . don't ask me,' Ross stammered, and walked quickly away.

'A fine display that was,' Angie said sarcastically as soon as they were out of earshot. 'And you accused me of taking orders from my mother!'

Ross, blushing scarlet, stopped in the middle of the pavement and smiled at her sheepishly. 'I suppose I did act a bit like Nigel there,' he admitted. 'So what do we do, go back and give her some moral support?'

Angie shook her head. 'No, one problem parent's probably enough.'

They turned into their own street and a heavy lorry clattered past. As the engine noise died away, a quavery voice could just be heard, carried in their direction by the afternoon breeze.

'Hold on,' Ross said, listening, 'that sounds like Jack.'

There was a lull in the traffic and the childish song came to them quite clearly:

15

> *Dame, what makes your ducks to die,*
> *Ducks to die, ducks to die;*
> *Dame, what makes your ducks to die ...?*

A car thudded past, but they caught most of the final verse:

> *Cannot fly, cannot fly;*
> *Their wings are cut and they cannot fly,*
> *On Christmas day in the morning.*

'Does he always sing nursery rhymes?' Angie asked.

'Only when there's something up. Let's take a look.'

They crossed the road and hurried down the narrow alley-way, reaching the lane behind the row of cottages just as Jack emerged from the field. He was bent over and staggering slightly from the weight of a sack slung across one shoulder.

'What's the matter, Jack?' Ross asked.

He peered at them suspiciously. 'Calling, that's what he was doing,' he murmured. 'Singing, sweeter than a flute. Old Jack heard him.'

'Who was doing the singing, Jack?'

But he refused to answer, shuffling past them, making for the shack at the end of the lane. It had been his home for as long as Ross could remember: a tumbledown three-roomed hut set in a tiny square of garden. Even at the best of times the garden was overgrown. Now it was a riot of plant life, with bindweed and elder and blackberry all knotted together.

Jack stopped at the edge of this tangled growth and upended his sack. At least a score of birds came spilling out: thrushes, blackbirds, rooks, a hawk, a pheasant, and several other species – the lifeless bodies tumbling over each other.

Angie bent down and touched the still, feathered bodies. 'Where did you find them, Jack?' she asked.

But again he refused to answer, entering his hut for a moment and reappearing with a rusty spade.

'Bury them,' he mumbled, 'where they can't hear. That's the

ticket.'

He made a feeble attempt to drive the spade into the ground, and Ross took it from him and set about digging a hole. When it was deep enough, he scooped the dead birds into it and filled it in.

'All right, Jack,' he said, leaning on the spade, 'now tell us what happened to them. How did they die?'

He started to sing again:

> *Their wings are cut and they cannot fly,*
> *Cannot fly . . .*

'No, Jack, not the song. Tell us what you know.'

The old man took off his hat and ruffled his wispy hair, making it stand out around his head like a halo. 'Sang to them, he did,' he said confidentially, 'called them.'

'What for?' Angie asked.

'But they couldn't have been any good, could they? I mean, look at them now.'

He stepped onto the grave and began to perform a sad little dance, his cracked leather shoes shuffling to and fro, his long threadbare overcoat swinging rhythmically about his heels.

'What might they have been good for, Jack?'

But he continued with his dance. 'Good for nothing now,' he muttered. 'Gone away. Stone deaf if he calls again.'

Ross glanced at Angie. 'I think we're wasting our time here.'

'Afraid so.'

'See you then, Jack.'

They began walking along the lane, but Jack called after them: 'If he sings to you, don't you listen.'

He picked up the spade and scraped ineffectually at the loose earth. 'Take some of the feathers. Stuff them in your ears. They won't need them. They won't listen again. Not them.'

FOUR

'I'm off, then.'

Bill Miller was standing in the front doorway of the cottage, a scarf knotted at his throat, his cap set at a rakish angle. 'You know where you can find me if you need to,' he said.

'Yes, enjoy yourself,' Ross said half-heartedly.

But the door had already closed.

Ross lingered by the window, staring out into the dusk. Then, with an impatient shrug of the shoulders, he went to turn on the television.

That was when he felt it again. Just as he was reaching for the switch the atmosphere in the room underwent a change, the former stillness of the evening suddenly replaced by a strange feeling of unrest, as if the air itself were trembling and alive. He remained exactly where he was, all his senses alert, aware of a faint tingling in his spine which seemed to travel slowly upwards and explode into his head in a wave of sound. Sweet as a flute, Jack had called it. And in those first few seconds he knew exactly what Jack had meant. A high undulating note, oddly melodious, like a soft and haunting song played on ancient reed pipes.

After that first conscious response he didn't think about the music again. It was merely there – a green-tinged path of light and sound along which he had to move. Everything else drab, dim. This one narrow corridor of incandescent green all that

18

really mattered; its softly glowing depths, pulsing gently to the rhythm of the song, beckoning to him.

With deliberate movements, he walked through the back garden. As he stepped outside, Angie emerged from the neighbouring cottage. Neither spared the other a glance, each wearing the same rapt expression. Behind them, unheeded, angry voices called out.

'Where do you think you're off to, my girl?'

'Angie? Didn't you hear your mother?'

'It's that Miller boy, George. Like father, like son. Tell her I won't have her . . .'

By then Angie had opened the garden gate, entering the lane just ahead of Ross, both of them walking away into the gathering darkness – except that for them the darkness barely existed; their attention riveted on the glowing path or tunnel, its faintly greenish tones as soft and muted as the music which created it.

Some way ahead there was a flicker of movement as Jack left his shack and came to meet them. He appeared at first to be in some distress, advancing with a reluctant, jerky kind of run, his mouth opening and closing soundlessly, his arms waving about as though he were struggling with some unseen presence. Once he stumbled to his knees, his arms flailing wildly. With some difficulty he scrambled up, crashed heavily against the side fence – and then, as he reached out to steady himself, grew suddenly calm, his silent struggle over. Now, his head sunk between his shoulders, his eyes staring straight before him, he too began to walk along the lane, his movements as mechanical as those of the children.

He was the first to reach the opening, and Angie and Ross followed him as he struck out across the field. None of them spoke. In Indian file they forced their way through the long grass, oblivious of the thistles and briars which tore at their skin and clothing, intent only on obeying the summons of the music. It grew louder as they neared the far side of the field, and Jack, his face still an impassive mask, burst involuntarily into song, his simple piping voice and the richer cadences which filled the night intertwining uneasily:

> *Oranges and lemons,*
> *Say the bells of St Clement's.*
> *You owe me five farthings,*
> *Say the bells of ... St Martin's.*
> *When will you pay ...?*

They were into the trees now, having to claw a passage through thick undergrowth – damp leaves brushing across their mouths, sticky strands of spiders' webs catching in their hair.

> *When ... will you ... pay ...?*

Invisible tendrils coiled about their legs, tripping them; branches and bushes lay in wait for them, as though intentionally barring their way; lustreless pools of nettles swayed forward at their approach, stinging their arms and cheeks. And through the gaps in the trees overhead, the cold eyes of stars observed their progress. Yet somehow, in spite of the difficulties, Jack continued with his song, the words, punctuated by wheezing gasps, bursting out in barely coherent snatches:

> *When I grow ... I grow ...*

He fell sprawling in a patch of chest-high ferns, Ross and Angie crashing into him.

> *Say the bells ...*

They rose and staggered on.

> *When will that be ... when ...?*

His voice rising, cracking slightly, as the music increased steadily in volume and intensity.

> *I'm sure I don't know ... sure ...*

They came to a halt, faced with a wall of leaves and stems, an obscuring screen that resisted all their initial attempts to push it down.

Says the great bell ... the great ... bell ...

With a concerted effort they heaved it aside, trampling through a smother of clinging green and breaking out into open space. Trees and bushes still crowded in from every side, but overhead the dark sky, with its cold pinpricks of light, was clearly visible. They stopped together – a fourth figure, unnoticed, sidling up from behind.

The source of the music felt close at hand, the strange melody louder and more urgent than ever. Yet now it was no longer soothing, or enticing. Ross felt as though he were being suffocated by it: the notes twining about his head, entering his eyes, his ears, his mouth, his nose, green tendrils of melody coiling within his skull. And in the distant background, Jack's voice, thin, reed-like, persistent:

I'm sure ... I don't know ...

Ross threw back his head, fighting for breath – dimly conscious of Angie groaning beside him.

Says the ... says the ...

The notes, still growing in volume, drew closer together, jarring against each other. There was no way of resisting their clamour and urgency. They filled his head, deafening, blinding him, closing him off from everything else, a wild tangle of shrill, mind-piercing sounds that built up and up unbearably. Somewhere in the midst of all that shrieking music, he was aware of a single incisive note, a sharp cutting edge of sound, that was reaching into the deepest, most secret parts of his mind, searching. Swiftly, surely, like a thin probing knife, it located the place it sought, and instantly he experienced a searing pain in his head, as of something burning, slicing through the soft quiver-

21

ing tissue of his brain. He didn't hear himself cry out in agony, the pain too intense for that – the music and the searing pain combining now, uniting in a final clanging discord that suddenly shattered into silence.

He didn't fall at once. For a few dazed seconds he stood swaying almost drunkenly in the shadowy stillness of the wood. Above him the circle of black sky wheeled and swung; the earth heaved convulsively beneath his feet. And with a desolate whimper he toppled forward, his eyes staring sightlessly into the gloom, his head pressed against the cool silence of the earth.

FIVE

He felt as though he were being watched, and he glanced up through the tall blades of grass and saw the moon peering over the edge of the trees. Its pale uncomforting light reminded him of how cold he was, and he rolled over and sat up, chafing his arms to increase the circulation. Only a pace or two away, Angie, her face hidden in shadow, was sitting with her arms clasped around her shoulders.

'Angie,' he whispered.

She crawled towards him, her teeth chattering. 'You all right?' she asked.

'I think so. What was all that about?'

'I don't know. But at least the music has stopped.'

'I'm not sure it has,' he said cautiously.

She understood immediately what he meant. The actual music was no longer audible, but there was still a vibrant quality about the night, the atmosphere somehow brittle, charged with a kind of static electricity, as though the melody were continuing at a level to which their ears were no longer attuned. Angie glanced nervously at the surrounding shadows, the tall trees, silent and still, looming up like threatening giants on all sides.

'If the music hasn't stopped,' she said, her voice dropping to a nervous whisper, 'why can't we hear it?'

Ross put both hands to his temples: the sharp, burning pain had gone, but still he retained a vivid memory of it. 'There was a hot feeling in my head,' he murmured. 'Did you feel it too?'

She nodded.

'Well maybe that's it,' he went on, 'maybe whatever's causing the music decided it didn't want us after all. So it did something to the inside of our heads, to stop us hearing it.'

'That's possible. I know sounds can deafen you if they're loud enough.'

'And some of the notes,' he added, 'they really hurt towards the end, as if they were trying to burn out a part of our brains.'

'You mean like burning out a circuit in a radio?'

'Something like that.'

The mere thought of such a possibility made them draw closer together in the chill night air.

'So what now?' she asked in a frightened, uncertain voice.

'The best thing we can do is clear out.'

He took her hand and half rose, but she held back.

'D'you think we're free to leave?' she whispered, again eyeing the surrounding trees nervously.

'Why not?' he replied with feigned carelessness. 'If we're right about what happened, the music can't affect us any more.'

'There's still whatever made the music. That might try and stop us.'

He shook his head, resisting the temptation to glance uneasily behind him. 'It may not be able to. Remember the animals the other day? Once they were back on their feet they just ran off. If they're anything to go by, there's nothing to keep us here now.'

She looked sharply at him. 'Are you saying we're being treated the same as those animals?'

'Well, aren't we?'

'But we're ...' She broke off, startled by a snuffling sound close by. 'What's that?'

24

Moving quietly to his left, Ross parted the long grass – only to reveal the pyjama-clad figure of Nigel. He was shivering with cold and fright, his cheeks smudged with tears.

'I might have known it'd be the shrimp,' Ross said with relief.

They hauled him out into the open and he stood limply between them. Without his glasses, his face looked more thin and pinched than ever.

'You're not a pretty sight,' Ross assured him, 'but better than some thing' I could have imagined.'

Nigel sniffed and wiped his nose on his cuff. 'What did you bring me here for?' he whimpered.

'Nobody brought you, Nigel,' Ross said. 'You walked.'

'But I haven't got any shoes on.'

'Well I certainly didn't carry you.'

'Go easy on him,' Angie said. 'He looks a bit shocked.'

'No, I'm not,' Nigel said petulantly, 'I'm freezing.'

'That makes three of us,' Ross cut in. 'Time we headed for home.'

With Nigel almost treading on their heels, they began groping their way back through the dense woodland. To begin with, Ross felt tense and uneasy. In spite of what he had said to Angie, about the music no longer having any hold over them, he kept expecting the strange, flute-like melody to break out again, to draw them back into the same sinister green tunnel that had lured them from their homes. But although the vibrant feeling in the air remained, it never approached the level of sound, and they reached the edge of the wood unmolested.

They could see the lights of the cottages now, and before they were half way across the field Nigel started to run. Ross grabbed him by the collar and pulled him back.

'A word of warning, Shrimp,' he said. 'Don't let on to your mother about the music. She'll think you're off your head – or more so than usual.'

Nigel looked at him with startled eyes. 'Music? What

25

music?'

'Come off it, Nigel. You know what I'm talking about.'

'I didn't hear any music,' he insisted in a high, almost hysterical voice. 'Honest, Ross. I just followed you.'

'All right, have it your way.'

He let him go, and Nigel raced off towards the lighted windows. Ross and Angie walked on more slowly, pausing at the opening to the lane.

'Do you believe him?' Angie asked.

'No way! Nigel's scared of his own shadow. He wouldn't have gone out there unless he'd had to.'

'So why did he lie?'

'For the same reason – he's scared. He'd much rather pretend nothing happened.'

'But if he really heard that music, how many other people did?'

'Probably no one beyond the lane, otherwise the woods would have been full of people.'

'We're the only ones then?'

Ross pursed his lips. 'Jack might have heard it too. It's all a bit vague now, but I seem to remember he was with us at one point.'

'Yes, so do I. And come to think of it, that sort of fits in. First something signals to the animals and birds in the area. Then, a few days later, it contacts the young people.'

'Jack's not exactly young.'

'He's not what you'd call an adult either.'

'I see what you're getting at.'

'But if he was out there,' Angie added, 'where's he got to?'

'With any luck, he's home already. Let's try the shack.'

They approached the unlit building and knocked tentatively. There was no answer and Ross pushed open the door and groped for the light switch. In the glare of the unshaded bulb the main room looked bare but surprisingly neat – the old iron bedstead carefully made up, the rickety pine table and the apple boxes, stacked to form a cupboard, covered with squares of faded cloth. Yet there was no sign of Jack.

Ross turned off the light and closed the door. 'He must still be out there,' he said with a frown. 'Alone.'

'Perhaps we should search for him.'

'There's no point. We'd never find him in the dark.'

In glum silence they walked slowly down the lane. Not until they had almost reached their own gardens did they become aware of the austere figure of Mrs Bowles waiting for them in the shadows.

'I'm surprised you have the nerve to show your face,' she said sharply, 'enticing my daughter away at all hours.'

'Mum, it wasn't Ross's fault,' Angie said.

'You keep out of this, my girl. Mr Hughes at the shop warned me to expect this kind of thing. Just like his father, he said.'

'But I'm trying to tell you ...'

'I don't need any telling. Your father and I saw the two of you sneaking off.'

'It wasn't like that!' Angie said in an outraged voice.

'I know what it was like. And I don't want you seeing him again. Otherwise we'll have you running as wild as he is.'

'Oh for god's sake!' Ross burst out.

He strode up the garden and went inside, slamming the door behind him.

'Stupid old bag!' he muttered.

Yet his resentment, real enough in itself, failed at that moment to touch him very deeply. Beneath his anger there persisted a much stronger concern for Jack. He stood quite still in the darkness, listening, wondering what might have happened to the old man. The house was quiet, the silence accentuating the electric feeling which seemed to charge the air all about him. What was it there for, he wondered. It was no longer an actual sound – not for him. But what of Jack? Did he perhaps still hear it as music? Was he wandering around out there somewhere, lured on by it? And for what purpose?

Ross shook his head as a burst of raucous singing issued from the street. Seconds later the front door crashed open and his father lurched into the entrance hall. He stood there in the shadows, his bulky figure swaying from side to side.

'Did you hear that?' he said in a slurred, self-important voice. 'Well that, my boy, is what you call real music.'

SIX

He wasn't sure whether he had been asleep or not, or even whether he had slipped into a vivid dream. The room was dark except for a pool of moonlight beneath the window, the lace curtain stirring gently in the current of cool air. Beside him, faintly luminous in the darkness, the alarm clock ticked vigorously. In the next room his father rolled over in a swish of bed clothes, took a few deep breaths, and resumed his loud snoring.

Ross sat up, swinging his feet out of bed, down onto the lino. The cold touch of it jolted him and he heard again the distant voice that had penetrated the familiar night-time sounds of the cottage and woken him.

Padding across to the window, he pulled aside the lace curtain and looked out. The profusion of growth in the narrow garden below appeared almost black in the moonlight. The lane, bordered on both sides by wooden fences, was equally dark and forbidding. As far as he could judge, it was empty. Yet the voice, a little nearer now, was unmistakable:

> ... *a chopper to chop off your head,*
> *Chip-chop, chip-chop, chip-chop.*

'Jack,' he murmured, relieved, his breath making a misty patch on the glass.

29

He rubbed it clear and detected a movement in the lane. A dark figure slid into view, keeping close to the fence.

Here comes a candle to light you to bed,
Here comes a . . .

Ross recognized the words easily enough, but the tune was wrong: not the familiar jingle he knew, but a weird, elusive melody. He eased the window open and leaned out.

'Jack!' he called in a loud whisper.

The dark figure made no response. Hatless, the bald dome of his head reflecting the moonlight, he edged through the half-open gate and sidled over to the wooden shed at the end of the garden. He disappeared inside and there was a rattle and bang of things being shoved around. Then he emerged, holding something that glinted in his hand.

. . . a chopper . . . a chopper . . . to chop . . .

'Hey, Jack, it's me!' – calling as loudly as he dared.

. . . to chop off . . . your head . . . your head . . .

The old man edged back through the gateway, his stooped figure flitting quickly down the lane, dissolving into the moon-streaked shadows.

Chip-chop, chip-chop . . .

Ross had to make up his mind rapidly. Pulling on a pair of rubber-soled shoes and a woollen jersey, he ducked through the open window and lowered himself onto the slanting roof of the kitchen. Above him and to his left was the window of Angie's room. He thought fleetingly of tapping on the glass, of waking her. But there was no time, Jack's voice already fading. Feet first, he slid down the smooth slate, swung himself out over the guttering, and dropped lightly to the ground.

Jack's singing had died away altogether now, and Ross hurried from the garden. At the entrance to the field he paused and scanned the open space, but nothing moved between him and the black line of trees, and he ran on as far as Jack's tumbledown hut.

It was still in darkness, the walls half buried in a welter of undergrowth, the sagging roof outlined against the star-speckled sky. Ross stood outside, unsure of which way to go next. Apart from the field, there was only the alleyway which led towards the village. It seemed an unlikely direction for Jack to have taken, and yet where else was there? He turned towards the alleyway – and then stopped.

. . . a chopper to chop . . . to chop . . .

The voice was strangely hesitant, faltering. It came from somewhere behind the hut and was followed by a series of tearing noises, as of someone cutting through bramble. Quickly, Ross entered the hut and groped his way through to the back door which stood wide open.

Jack was standing in the garden. He must have been clearing a space because he was festooned with tendrils of bindweed and wild hop. A strong smell of sap filled the air. He still held the axe in his right hand, while with his left he was sweeping aside the fallen stems and leaves, revealing the scarred surface of a chopping block.

'You all right, Jack?' Ross asked.

The old man did not turn or look up. Kneeling amongst the grass and hacked-down plants, he placed his left hand deliberately on the block and raised the axe.

Here comes a chopper to chop . . .

'No!' Ross shouted.

He leaped forward, but not before the axe had descended. He saw the gnarled index finger separate itself from the rest of the hand, roll across the block, and teeter on the edge; and then he was holding Jack, steadying him as he rocked from side to side.

31

'*Chip-chop, chip-chop ...*' he moaned.

'I've got you, I've got you,' Ross murmured, too shocked to take in what had happened.

Yet the sight of the chopping block, with its dark stain and grisly burden, soon brought home to him the urgency of the situation. Tugging at the old man's bony shoulder, he tried to heave him to his feet.

'Come on!' he said desperately. 'A hospital's what you need.'

But Jack pushed him away. '*Chip-chop ...*' he moaned again.

Dropping the axe, he snatched at the severed finger, grasping it in his good hand. 'Go now,' he said in a flat, dead voice, 'go ...'

He stood up slowly. The gaping wound in his left hand was pouring with blood, a dark stain which ran down over his wrist, soaking the sleeve of his overcoat. But his face was calm, expressionless, revealing no hint of pain – his eyes a dull black, strangely unseeing.

'Go now,' he repeated mechanically, and shouldered Ross aside, stumbling through the darkened hut.

Ross followed him only as far as the front door. Clicking on the light, he looked wildly around the main room. His eye fell on the apple-box cupboard, and he tore aside the cloth screen and peered inside. In one of the compartments, neatly stacked, was a pile of white handkerchiefs. Scooping them up, he hurried off in pursuit of the old man, catching him up just as he was about to enter the field. He was still gripping the severed finger in his right hand, holding on to it as if his life depended on its preservation. Again he tried to push past Ross, his eyes dully reflecting the moonlight. Only when Ross stood firm did he pause briefly, his feet shuffling restlessly on the gravelly surface of the lane.

'Here,' Ross said, and took the damaged hand in both of his.

He winced when he saw the wound close up and quickly

clamped a thick wad of handkerchiefs onto it. With the other handkerchiefs he held the wad firmly in place, looping them over the hand and knotting them tightly around the wrist. While he worked, Jack made no attempt to break free; but as soon as he had finished, the old man lurched away.

'Don't be a fool!' Ross cried out, grabbing at him.

'No!' Jack protested, 'no!'

His ravaged face was suddenly twisted with emotion, as though he were engaged in some struggle with himself.

'What is it, Jack?'

A gleam of intelligence entered the dull eyes. 'Listen,' he faltered out, 'listen to . . .'

'Is it the music? Can you still hear it?'

But the brief gleam had already died. He jerked his arm, trying to shake free. And when that failed, moving with a speed which completely belied his age, he swung his fist in a short, vicious arc, catching Ross on the temple and sending him sprawling.

For a minute or two Ross was aware only of an overwhelming dizziness. He tried to rise, found he had no control over his limbs, and toppled forward onto his face and chest. There was grass in his mouth, live green stems pressing against his tongue, his palate, choking him. He coughed and spat them out, forcing himself up into a sitting position. Gradually his vision cleared, the world tilting back into place, and with one hand on his painfully throbbing temple he clambered to his feet.

The field, as he had feared, was empty.

'I know you're out there, Jack,' he called.

There was no answer – the shadowy grass, the moonlit curve of the sky, the distant line of trees absorbing the sound of his voice and giving nothing in return. Somewhere behind him a dog started to bark, the regular yap-yap keeping time with the throbbing in his head.

'It's no good hiding,' he yelled. 'I'll find you.'

But he knew it was an empty threat – the darkness and the

dense woodland offering Jack perfect cover.

Reluctantly, he made for home. With the help of the drain-pipe and the kitchen window-sill, he climbed onto the roof and slipped back into his room. Everything was as he had left it: the rumpled bed clothes, the regular ticking of the clock, his father's half-strangled snores on the other side of the wall. Dragging a blanket from the bed, he draped it over his shoulders and stationed himself by the open window. From there he had a clear view of the field. Even with the moon low in the sky, no one could possibly come or go without ...

He turned his head sharply and listened, thinking for a moment that the clock had stopped. Then, all at once, he realized what had happened. The air was still at last; that constant soundless hum, so persistent that he had come almost to ignore it, no longer there. In its absence a brief, heavy silence descended on the night – shattered almost immediately by a faint yet undeniable scream. A scream, Ross felt sure, which originated somewhere in the distant woodland.

SEVEN

'He did what?' Angie asked, her eyes round with shock.

'I've told you, he ...'

'No, don't say it again!'

They were standing at the far edge of the playground. All around them children were playing or talking together in small groups. A keen spring wind was blowing, ruffling the mass of ivy which coiled up the side of the school building and had begun to creep across the roof.

'Not talking about it won't alter anything,' Ross said.

'But the thought of him actually ...' She shuddered, closing her eyes tightly.

'Watch out,' Ross murmured, 'here's the local heavy.'

A teacher, coffee mug in hand, sauntered towards them. 'Anything the matter, Angie?'

'The matter, Sir?' – her shocked expression changing to one of wide-eyed innocence.

'Miller here not bothering you, is he?'

'No, Sir. Should he be?'

'It's not beyond his capacity. Isn't that right, Miller?'

'If you say so, Sir.'

The teacher scowled, sipped at his coffee, and strolled on.

'Stupid creep!' Ross muttered.

The troubled look had returned to Angie's face. 'So where's

Jack now?' she asked.

'Still in the woods, I expect. I checked his hut this morning, and the bed hadn't been slept in.'

'But he could die with a wound like that!'

'He might if we don't find him.'

She turned her back abruptly on the noise of the playground. Beyond the nearest row of houses, the bare swell of the downs was just visible, the treeless horizon forming a curving line against the white of the clouds. The breeze, blowing into their faces, carried the fitful sound of traffic from the highway which bordered the village.

'Shouldn't we report the whole thing to the police?' she suggested hopefully.

'Don't be crazy! What would we tell them? That Pan was playing his pipes in the wood?'

'No, only about Jack.'

'Oh great! And give them an excuse to stick him away! What old Hughes has always wanted.'

Behind them the bell began ringing. The shouting and laughter faltered as games broke up and groups of children made their way towards the main entrance.

'I could come after school,' she said hesitantly.

'You know that'd be too late. It has to be now.'

The playground was emptying rapidly and they also headed for the school building. Angie swept her hair away from her face with a nervous gesture.

'There'll be hell to pay if we're caught,' she said. 'Not only here. At home too. Mum'll start ringing the welfare people if I know her.'

'We'll have to make sure we're not caught.'

The last stragglers were already pushing through the glass doors, and Ross took Angie's hand and drew her around the side of the building. They flattened themselves against the wall, almost disappearing in the dense growth of ivy. Ross had the eery sensation that he could feel it growing, coiling against his back.

'Give them a minute to settle down,' he whispered.

The main door swished open and closed and Nigel poked his head around the corner. 'What are you up to?'

'Get lost, Shrimp.'

'If you're dodging school, can I come with you?'

Ross pulled him roughly into the shelter of the ivy. 'Just answer one thing, Shrimp. Have you remembered about last night yet? You know, the music?'

A frightened, defensive look came into Nigel's eyes. 'I've already told you,' he whined, 'I didn't hear anything.'

'Well that's bad luck, because you can only come with us when your memory improves.'

Ross shoved him away contemptuously and they heard the doors swish closed as he scurried back inside.

'Come on,' Ross said and walked towards the gate.

Angie started to run, but he cautioned her to slow down. 'Keep it to a walk and no one'll notice a thing.'

She gave him a nervous smile. 'I can see you've done this before.'

'You'll get used to it.'

'I hope not.'

The hair on the back of her neck was tingling unpleasantly and she braced herself for the sound of a voice. But nobody called out, and minutes later they were well clear of the school.

They broke into a run then, hurrying along Elm Walk – the once gaunt trees now covered with a haze of green shoots – and down the narrow alleyway to Jack's hut. It still appeared deserted, but to make doubly sure they went through to the back.

Angie, unnerved by the thought of what had so recently happened there, lingered just inside the scullery door. 'Is that the chopping block?' she asked.

'Yes, you can still see . . .' He stopped and peered at it more closely. 'That's funny. Look at this.'

He pointed to the scarred surface of the block. The bloodstain was still visible, but scrawled across it, in chalk, was a simple cross; and at the centre of the cross was a small heap of gravel.

'Someone's been here,' he said. 'Maybe Jack.'

A disturbing idea occurred to Angie. 'You said he dropped the axe. Where is it now?'

Ross felt around in the grass. 'It's gone.'

'Are you sure?'

Overcoming her instinctive reluctance, she helped him search. They found nothing.

'You don't think . . .?' she began in a frightened tone.

There was no need to finish, the two of them already scrambling back through the hut and out into the lane.

'This way,' Ross said.

They climbed over the fence and ran straight across the field, crouching low in the hope of not being seen from the cottages. At the far side they checked hurriedly along the edge of the woodland, but the only obvious break in the wall of foliage was the one they had made the previous evening.

'It'll have to do,' Angie said.

They had no difficulty in following their own trail, stopping every twenty or thirty paces to call out. The gusty wind carried their voices through the trees, but there was no reply, and before long they reached the end of the trail and stood again in the small clearing.

By day it looked different, not nearly as hemmed in as they had imagined, actually part of a large hollow which was altogether less overgrown than the surrounding woodland. At its lowest point the hollow was dominated by two enormous trees: a giant elm and a towering pine, the tips of their branches intertwining.

'Seems we've drawn a blank,' Angie said.

'I don't think so.'

Ross plucked a blade of grass and held it out to her. One side of the spear-like tip was darkly stained with blood.

'So he's been here!'

With renewed energy they circled the hollow, searching for signs of a fresh trail leading on; but again they drew a blank.

'Either he's hiding down there somewhere,' Angie said, 'or he's gone back the way he came.'

Ross nodded, eyeing the hollow suspiciously. 'You know, something about this place worries me,' he said, 'something that isn't quite right.'

'It's strange the way we've been drawn back here, if that's what you mean.'

'Not only that. The place itself. It's wrong somehow.'

'Sort of scary?'

'Not that either. It's more like . . .'

'Like what?'

He shook his head, puzzled. 'I'm not really sure. Maybe it's my imagination. Anyway, we're wasting time.'

They worked their way down the slope, searching as they went. Initially they found nothing unusual, but at the very bottom of the hollow they pulled up with a start. It was exactly as if a small portion of the woodland had been attacked. Stems of saplings and bushes were chopped through; limbs had been lopped off sturdier trees; and the massive trunks of the elm and the pine had been hacked about with an axe. The pine especially was badly scarred.

'Who could have done a thing like that?' Angie said.

Ross went closer to the pine. Running the length of the trunk was a black scorch mark where the tree had recently been damaged by lightning. Yet it wasn't that wound which bothered Ross now. With a pained expression, he slipped his fingers into one of the numerous axe cuts.

'By the look of things,' he said unhappily, 'Jack went crazy. But why?'

Angie picked up one of the fallen limbs. It had been cut off cleanly, as if by a single stroke. 'You have to be either very strong or very angry to do this,' she said. 'And a little old man like Jack can't be very strong.'

Ross nodded. 'I agree, he must have been angry. But what with? Senseless plants?'

'No, probably not.'

'What then?'

'Well, you admitted yourself that he was in some kind of trance when he chopped off his finger. Something must have been controlling him.'

'The way the music controlled us earlier?'

'Sort of. And when Jack came to, he decided that whatever was causing all the trouble was hiding around here. So he got the axe and did this.'

'Revenge?'

'I think so.'

'But why take his feelings out on plants?'

'Maybe that isn't what he was trying to do. He might have been after something else, that he couldn't see or touch. All this' – she indicated the surrounding trees – 'just happened to be in the way.'

Ross ran his hand thoughtfully over the scarred surface of the pine. 'Poor old Jack,' he said. 'He must have been desperate.'

'I expect he was.'

'But he's always been so gentle. That's the great thing about him. And now for him to suddenly go and . . . ' He took a deep breath. 'We might as well head for home. In that state of mind he could have run off anywhere.'

He began to trudge up the slope. 'You coming?'

She didn't move. Waiting until he paused and glanced back. 'What we need is some kind of clue,' she said. 'A message from Jack himself.'

Ross gazed at her, mystified. 'A message? But he doesn't even know how to write.'

'That's the point. People who can't write usually sign their

40

names with a cross.'

'A cross?'

'Yes.'

The frown of bewilderment suddenly cleared from his face.

'Like . . . like the cross on the chopping block?'

'I think that's where he left the message,' she said.

EIGHT

'But why did he choose to put it here?' Angie asked.

She touched the chalk mark on the level surface of the block, taking care to avoid the bloodstain – she and Ross facing each other in the small garden.

'He must have guessed this is where we'd look for him,' Ross replied.

'He'd have stood a better chance of attracting our attention if he'd scrawled it on the fence or the front wall of the hut.'

'Perhaps he wasn't thinking too clearly at the time.'

Angie leaned forward, an intent expression on her face. 'Either that, or he knew exactly what he was up to.Couldn't it have been deliberate? After all, this is the one place he had every reason to avoid, after what had happened to him. By leaving his mark here, he might have been trying to tell us things were under control and he wasn't panicking any more.'

Ross considered the idea. 'It sounds a bit subtle for Jack.'

'But you're the one who says he isn't really mad – that he's just a dropout.'

'Even so . . .'

'All right,' she went on quickly, 'let's leave that. There's still the fact that he made his mark with a piece of chalk.'

'You reckon that's important?'

'After what Jack went through, yes, I do.'

'How can a piece of chalk tie in with anything?'

'I don't know yet, but let's try putting ourselves in Jack's position. He obviously realized that something out there in the woods had been controlling him. In that situation, what would we have done?'

'What we did last night – got the hell out of there.'

'Yes, but if we were really scared, where would we have gone? You know this area better than I do.'

A gleam of awakening excitement began to show in Ross's eyes. 'Wait a minute,' he said, 'I think you're on to something. In Jack's place I'd have stayed well clear of the woods. Got as far away as I could.'

'Go on.'

Ross drew in his breath sharply. 'Yes, that's it! What he must have done! Headed for the downs!'

'Why there?'

Ross pointed meaningfully at the chalk mark. 'Because the downs are mainly chalk, with just a layer of grass over the top.'

'That's probably where he is then,' Angie agreed, the relief clearly audible in her voice.

'The downs are pretty big though,' Ross reminded her. 'It might take us days to find him.'

He stood up, as if about to leave.

'Hold on,' Angie said, 'we haven't finished with his message yet. There's still the heap of gravel he left here. That must mean something.'

Ross looked down at the bloodstained block. 'Any ideas?'

'Well for a start, X could be more than just his name. It could also be the kind of cross used to mark an important spot on a map. And the gravel's been placed right on that spot.'

Ross dropped to his knees and made a close inspection of the carefully arranged heap of stones. 'It was put there deliberately all right,' he said. 'You can see that. But what's it doing there?'

Angie smiled weakly at him. 'That's what I was hoping you could tell me.' She pulled thoughtfully at her lower lip. 'Let's go back to the beginning again. The chalk suggested the downs. So what does gravel suggest? Roadworks, maybe, or a quarry . . .'

'A quarry!' Ross interrupted excitedly. 'There's an old disused quarry on the downs! That's where we'll find him!' He leaned back in the grass and grinned up at her. 'You know something? I never realized it before, but you're pretty bright.'

She reddened slightly and made a mock bow. 'For my next trick . . .'

'No, you really are.'

'Well, with my brains and your brawn . . .'

'Hey, don't go too far!' he said with a laugh.

But she had already grown more serious. 'Before we start congratulating ourselves,' she cautioned him, 'let's find out if we're right.'

Ross, equally serious now, rose quickly to his feet. 'We'd better be – for Jack's sake.'

NINE

The door banged closed behind him as Ross left the shop. Angie was waiting just around the corner, out of the wind.

'What did you get?' she asked.

He opened the mouth of the packet for her to peer inside. 'A roll of bandage, some lint pads, and antiseptic.'

'Did you have enough money?'

'I said it was for an educational project and asked her to charge it to the school.'

'And she agreed?'

'She wasn't too happy about it, but she did in the end.'

Angie groaned. 'The longer this goes on,' she said gloomily, 'the more trouble I see us getting into.'

'Not half as much trouble as Jack's in already.'

She looked at him carefully. 'You really care about Jack, don't you?'

'Somebody has to,' he said casually.

But she could detect the note of veiled concern in his voice.

'Well we can't help him by just standing around here,' she said.

Taking the shortest route from the village, they crossed the busy highway and set out across the downs. For the first ten minutes the sound of traffic along the highway engulfed them,

45

the noise amplified by the dish-shaped hillside. But the moment they topped the rise it was as if the highway had ceased to exist. There was only the moan of the wind and the downs stretching on towards the treeless horizon – a great sweep of open country, mainly bright green, but speckled with white by chalk outcrops.

'Is it always like this?' Angie asked, exhilarated by the sense of open space.

Ross bent to pick a spray of meadowsweet. 'It's always green in spring,' he said, 'but usually it's just grass. I've never seen so many flowers up here.'

They trudged on, their heads lowered against the wind, their feet swishing through the grass. At one stage Ross stopped and pointed back over the way they had come, to where the village nestled in the velvety lushness of the valley.

'Take a last look,' he said. 'We lose it after the next rise.'

With the village gone from view, the downs took on a more austere quality. The buttercups and meadowsweet, the bright scattering of daisies, vanished from the landscape, and all that remained were tough clumps of grass and the hard feel of chalk underfoot.

'This is more like it,' Ross shouted above the roar of the wind.

They pushed on for a while longer. Then, all at once – or so it seemed to Angie – the ground opened almost at their feet, and there beneath them was the quarry.

She had imagined it as a single hole in the ground, but it proved to be a series of deep pits backed by artificial hills or mounds, the whole complex extending over a large area. Many of the walls and cliff faces had caved in, creating a labyrinth of narrow valleys, the deepest of them filled with murky water. The entire area had been enclosed by a wire-mesh fence topped with barbed wire, and at the western extremity tall padlocked gates faced out onto a deeply rutted track.

'Where would he hide in a place like this?' Angie asked.

46

'I'll show you.'

He led the way down to the gates. A notice board had been bolted onto the metal frame, warning people that this was a dangerous area and to keep out. But with a knowing grin, he climbed over the gates and dropped down on the other side.

'I might have guessed it would be illegal,' Angie muttered as she clambered after him.

Once inside, they followed the overgrown track into the nearest of the valleys. Not far from the gates, the track turned abruptly, and they came upon a wooden shed huddled in the shelter of a crumbling cliff face. The windows were broken, the door hanging from its hinges, but otherwise it was in reasonable condition – the walls undamaged, the iron roof still intact. Set against one wall was a rusty fresh-water tank connected to the gutter by a metal pipe.

'Doesn't look too hopeful,' Angie began – and broke off as Jack's shadowy figure suddenly appeared within the dusty interior. Without warning, he leaped towards them, a flash and gleam of metal in his hand.

'Look out!' Ross yelled. He staggered backwards, away from the doorway, almost falling into Angie's arms, as something bright and heavy thudded harmlessly into the door jamb.

'He's crazy!' Angie cried.

But Ross, after the first shock, stood his ground. 'You want to be careful,' he said, speaking to Angie over his shoulder, 'you're beginning to sound like old Hughes.'

'I don't care whom I sound like! Just look at him!'

Jack was standing in the open doorway, his right hand clinging to the axe which was still embedded in the side timber. His face had a haggard, ghastly quality about it, his eyes red-rimmed and staring. His damaged left hand hung limply at his side, the blood-soaked handkerchiefs dried into a formless brown blob.

'He's not crazy,' Ross said quietly, 'just exhausted. He probably hasn't slept since the other night.'

He went up to Jack and gently disengaged the hand gripping

the axe. 'Are you tired, Jack?' he murmured soothingly. 'Do you want to lie down for a bit?'

'I thought ... I thought ...' he stammered, 'that you ...' He blinked rapidly several times and began to cry, the tears welling over the reddened lower lids and running down into the hollows of his cheeks. 'I thought ... when you ...'

'It's all right, Jack, we wouldn't have left you up here on your own.'

Ross put his arm protectively about the old man's shoulders and led him back into the shed, easing him down onto the low wooden pallet that stood in one corner. He lay back without protest, continuing to whimper like a child.

'We'd better see what we can do about his injury,' Angie said to Ross. 'Can you find something to put water in?'

Amongst the litter on the floor was a battered enamel bowl; and he took it outside, cleaned it as best he could, and half filled it with water from the tank. Placing it beside the makeshift bed, he stood behind Angie, watching her carefully remove the binding handkerchiefs. When only the blood-soaked pad remained, she hesitated.

'Should we soak it off?' she asked.

Jack lay quietly watching them, no longer crying.

'Better leave it as it is,' Ross advised. 'If you pull it off or get it wet, the wound will only start bleeding again.'

'But what about infection?'

'It's already bled a lot, which should help. And I think he's had enough pain and shock for a while.'

'All right, we'll take a chance.'

They cleaned the rest of the hand and then liberally sprinkled the existing pad with antiseptic, binding it up afterwards with the clean bandage. Before they had finished, Jack was sound asleep, breathing evenly. Ross took off his coat, laid it gently across the old man's chest, and tip-toed from the shed.

Angie was already waiting outside. 'We can't leave him like that,' she said. 'One of us'll have to fetch a doctor.'

But Ross shook his head. 'He's fine as he is for a while,' he replied stubbornly.

'How do you know?'

'I've already told you, if this got out – what he's done to himself – there are plenty of people who'd jump at the chance of sticking him in an asylum.'

'At least he'd be well taken care of.'

He turned on her angrily. 'Jack doesn't want to be taken care of! Not in that way! He just wants to live his own life and not fall into the hands of busybodies like Hughes.'

'Perhaps he nearly fell into the hands of something far worse,' she suggested.

'Perhaps he did. But isn't that why he came here? To get away? He could have gone anywhere – to a doctor, a hospital, the police – but he chose this place. Leave him in peace.'

'But what if he gets really ill? That wound might . . .'

'There you go again!' he broke in. 'Worrying about what hasn't happened yet! If he gets worse, that'll be the time to worry.'

'It might be too late by then.'

'And that'll be his choice too,' he retorted.

His voice had an angry ring to it, and she gave him a few minutes to simmer down. When he was calm, she said quietly, 'Tell me something. What's so special about Jack? Would you take the same trouble over your dad or someone like Nigel?'

'Nigel's just anybody.'

'And Jack?'

'He's different.'

'In what sense?'

'You're the bright one – work it out.'

'No, tell me.'

He ran his fingers through his hair. Above them, at ground level, the wind roared and sighed. 'There's no one quite like Jack. Without him, the whole village, the people in it, would be sort of nothing.'

49

'Nothing?'

'Not all of them maybe. But most of the adults. Robots. Exactly what Jack's never become.'

He picked up a piece of flint and threw it at the sheer face of the cliff. A shower of chalk fragments came bouncing down onto the heap of debris already gathered at the base.

'Then we'd better decide how to look after him while he's here,' Angie said.

TEN

He could hear Mrs Bowles' voice, shrill and unpleasant: 'I won't have this kind of thing happening again! I really must insist that he stays away from her!'

And then his father's reply, more of a threatening growl: 'Don't you insist with me! As far as I can see, she's the one who needs watching!'

'That, Mr Miller, is a matter of opinion!'

'Yes, and when I need your opinion I'll ask for it!'

The front door closed with a violence that shook the cottage, and Bill Miller came stomping through to the kitchen.

'What's this I hear?' he said angrily. 'Running off from school and then hanging around the streets with that brat next door! What's got into you? You soft on her or something?'

'No, it's not like that, Dad,' Ross said. 'And she's not a brat anyway.'

His father aimed a clumsy blow at his head and he dodged back out of reach. He was nearly as tall as his father, but not as heavy, and he knew the weight of that hand from long experience.

'Don't you bandy words with me, boy!' Bill Miller warned him. 'You keep away from her. Understand?'

'So you're taking sides with Mrs Bowles?'

'I'm taking sides with no one. I don't want trouble, that's all.

51

Now get upstairs before I really lose my temper.'

Ross edged along the wall of the kitchen, deftly avoiding another blow from that large callused hand, and ran upstairs. Down below, his father continued to march angrily to and fro, but Ross guessed that wouldn't last long – storms of this kind were usually short-lived. Meanwhile he was glad enough to be left alone. Everything else was ready – his rucksack packed with food and camping gear that afternoon – and all that remained was for him to get some rest.

Drawing the curtains, he slipped fully clothed into bed. As an afterthought he set the alarm clock and tucked it under his pillow. But it proved unnecessary because at half-past nine his father knocked at the door.

'You awake, son?'

He surfaced with a rush. 'Yes.'

'No hard feelings?' – the voice only slightly slurred.

'No. Just thought I'd have an early night.'

'Okay.'

The stairs creaked as his father went back to the television.

Ross, already up, was putting on his shoes and coat, dragging the rucksack from beneath the bed. He tapped on the intervening wall and climbed silently out onto the kitchen roof. Angie joined him there moments later.

'You'll have to go on your own tonight,' she whispered apologetically. 'Mum's watching me like a hawk. She's in and out of my room every ten minutes.'

'Oh well,' he said, doing his best to hide his disappointment.

'I'm sorry. Really.'

'Forget it. Things bad at home?'

'Pretty bad. Silences mostly. Mum's the worst.'

'How'd she find out?'

'Nigel told one of the teachers.'

'Little creep! Wait till I catch him!'

'It didn't matter though, because Mr Hughes spotted us crossing the field. He must have been watching from the shop window.'

'You see what I mean about that man,' he said bitterly.

'Never mind, it'll soon blow over. And I managed to get some food for Jack.'

She took a large packet from the window-sill, pushed it into the open mouth of the rucksack, and pulled the drawstring tight.

'Here, let me give you a hand with this,' she said.

He swung himself over the gutter and dropped to the ground. Angie handed the rucksack down to him. With the televisions turned on in both cottages, there was little chance of their being heard.

'I wish you were coming,' he said.

'So do I. Maybe I could just come a bit of the way.'

'No, better wait for things to quieten down.'

She waved awkwardly. 'Good luck, then.'

He shouldered the rucksack and set off, quickly traversing the silent village, reaching the highway just as the moon rose. He was glad of its thin clear light as he tramped across the deserted upland – it made him feel less lonely and nervous. But he was still relieved when the quarry came into sight.

Once over the gates, he approached the hut quietly and tiptoed inside. The moon, shining through the broken window, fell across Jack's sleeping face. Ross touched his forehead, noting with satisfaction that it was cool.

Taking care not to disturb the old man, he unpacked the rucksack, setting the things out neatly on the dusty floor. By the light of a candle, he started the spirit stove and put soup on to heat. He was stirring it when Jack woke.

'That you, Ross boy?'

He went over to the pallet. 'How're you doing?'

The old man tried to sit up, sighed, and sank back. 'You spotted it then,' he said with a chuckle. 'My little puzzler. Guessed you would. Read it off pat, I bet.'

He seemed unaware that Ross had been there before.

'That was pretty smart, Jack. As clear as if you'd written it with pencil and paper.'

'Aye. Not born yesterday. Old Jack takes some catching when his blood's up.'

He again struggled into a half sitting position, propping himself against the back wall, and began to chant in a sing-song voice:

> *Jack be nimble, Jack be quick,*
> *Jack jump over the candlestick.*

'Well don't jump over that one,' Ross said, indicating the candle in the corner. 'It's the only light we've got.'

Jack nodded happily. 'Knew you'd find your old mate. But not that other one. Bamboozle him, I thought. And sure enough I did.'

'Which other one?'

'Him, the green piper, the chip-chop chopper.'

'You saw him?'

'We'll all see him before long. Wicked devil that he is ... he is ...' He began to mumble and doze, his eyelids drooping shut.

'Here, let's have a look at that hand,' Ross said.

He brought the candle nearer and took off the bandage. The edge of the wound, which was all that he could see, appeared less swollen, and some of the ugly redness had disappeared.

'Is it sore?' he asked.

Jack started awake. 'He's the one who took it,' he said. 'Kept it.'

'Who?'

'Him. Tucked it away. Jack's pointer. His favourite.'

'But what would he want your finger for, Jack?'

'That'd be telling.'

'You can tell me.'

Jack closed one eye craftily. 'I'll tell you this:

54

A wise old owl lived in an oak,
The more he saw the less he spoke,
The less he spoke the more he heard,
Why can't we all be like that wise old bird?'

While he chanted, Ross replaced the bandage.

'And that's all you're saying?' he asked.

'Mum. That's the word.'

'Have it your own way. How about some food? Hungry?'

'Don't simple-simon me, Ross boy.'

'What's that mean?'

'There's not a penny for the pieman, nor a pie for the simple lad. Not here.'

'But I've brought food. There's soup cooking now.'

Jack's face broke into a toothless grin. 'Yum's the word. Empty as a cave. As them caves over past the wood.'

Ross poured the soup into a bowl, added some milk to cool it, and spooned it into Jack's mouth. He gulped down several spoonfuls, then lost interest, leaning his head back against the wall.

'Old Jack's tired ... tired ...'

He seemed to fall instantly into a deep sleep, and Ross eased him down and covered him with a blanket.

With nothing else to do now, he walked outside and stood in the middle of the valley. The wind had dropped, leaving the night calm and still. The moon was quite high already, casting silver-edged shadows along the base of the cliff. The chalk, where it wasn't in shadow, glowed a purplish-white. Overhead, the cloudless sky formed a blue-black dome, sprinkled unevenly with countless pin-pricks of light. Ross didn't move. After the worry and uncertainty of the past twenty-four hours, this lonely, isolated spot felt unexpectedly peaceful, secure, momentarily soothing his undefined fears. Here, far from the woodlands, Jack would be safe – safe from whatever had been hunting him. Which might give up now, might even ...

The silence was shattered by Jack's voice raised in terrified protest, 'Don't leave it for him! Don't! Not for him to read!'

He ran back into the shed. 'What's the matter, Jack?'

The old man was awake, his eyes staring into the shadows. 'The message! The puzzler! That I made for you! Don't leave it for him!'

He tried to roll off the bed, and Ross had to hold him down.

'Don't worry. Nobody's touched it.'

'No! Spoil it! Wipe it off! Promise me you will!'

'Yes, I promise,' he said placatingly. He felt Jack's body gradually relax.

'Because if you don't, he'll come. Scurrying like a rat.'

'Who are you talking about?'

'The hangman, the pieman, the chip-chop chopper. Him that deals in meat.'

'What's his real name, Jack?'

'Why, the green piper. That's what he whispered. Fluted it to me, he did. He'll be looking for yours truly later on. When his time comes. When he's ripe and ready. Won't tolerate a poor broken-down old man. A bag of bones, that's all. And him a dealer in meat, a dealer ...'

He drifted back into sleep. Ross felt his forehead, but there was no sign of fever.

'Rest now, Jack,' he murmured.

He again went outside. Nothing had changed – the quarry silent and still, windless, bathed in a soft pale light. Yet now the night felt neither peaceful nor secure. It was as if something were already lurking out there, waiting. The very shadows had acquired a sinister quality. They seemed to move imperceptibly, slowly closing in upon him, as though stirred into uneasy life by Jack's nameless terror. No – he corrected himself – not nameless. Jack had named the source of his fear. The green piper, a dealer in meat.

Ross glanced across at the hut. The axe was still there,

protruding from the door jamb, like a savage reminder.

'Rest now, Jack,' he repeated – setting those simple words of comfort against his suddenly awakened sense of dread.

PART II
SUMMER

ONE

The buzzer whirred as Ross entered the shop. Inside, it felt cool, almost cold, after the unrelenting heat of the day. Within the dim, slightly dusty interior he could see the overweight, dark-haired figure of Mr Hughes standing behind the counter. The shopkeeper glanced across at him, but said nothing, turning his attention back to Mrs Bowles who was slowly packing her purchases into a wicker basket.

Ross slipped between the lines of shelves and ran his eye quickly over the rows of tinned goods.

'... just everywhere,' Mrs Bowles was saying in her most injured tones, 'like a plague. And so dirty.'

'That's the part that bothers me,' Mr Hughes agreed, 'the dirt. In my line of business that's always a worry.'

'They haven't started to ...?' Mrs Bowles began.

'Oh no, not in here. But the garden and the field across the lane are full of them.'

'Yes, they even drink the cat's milk at the back step.'

Ross, half listening, saw what he was after on the top shelf. 'Spam,' Jack had said, licking his lips with relish, 'that's the thing I miss.' Ross took down two tins and walked over to the door. Under the pretext of gazing out, he slid one tin onto the shelf level with the door catch, pushing it behind a large packet of toilet rolls. When he turned back the shopkeeper was still talking, having noticed nothing unusual.

'There was a time,' he was murmuring confidentially, 'when I'd have blamed you-know-who in that shack at the end of the lane. A breeding ground, you might say. But with the change that's come over him recently ... well, I don't know.'

Mrs Bowles shook her head understandingly. 'Perhaps it's the heat that's brought them out. I've never known a year like this one.'

She looked around as Ross approached.

'Afternoon, Mrs Bowles.'

Her lips drew into a thin line of disapproval. 'I'll be off then,' she said, pointedly ignoring him.

Ross shrugged and pushed the tin across the counter. 'Just the spam today, please, Mr Hughes.'

The shopkeeper rang the amount up on the till and held out his hand for the money.

'Ah well ... that's the problem,' Ross stammered, with an elaborate show of being embarrassed, 'you see ...'

The big hand shot forward and scooped up the tin. 'I wasn't born yesterday, young Miller.'

'But I could pay you in a day or two. Honest.'

'I've heard that one before. I'm surprised you've got the cheek to come in here begging. Pity you don't take a leaf out of Jack's book.'

'Jack?'

'Yes, a big improvement, and I'm not the only one who's noticed it. Smartened himself up, dropped all that mad nonsense. I hardly recognize him as the same person.'

Ross frowned, wondering whether he was being made fun of. 'But you've always said Jack's not fit to live here.'

'Never mind what I've said,' Mr Hughes replied irritably. 'The man's made an effort at last, dressing and acting like other decent people. Anyone can see that. You should follow his example.'

'Jack's example?' Ross said, puzzled. 'You really mean

Jack?'

'Who else?'

'But Jack hasn't been seen in the village for ...'

He stopped, aware that the shopkeeper was barely listening. Waving a large beefy hand he signalled the end of their brief exchange.

'As this isn't a charitable institution,' he said sarcastically, ' I don't see that you and I have any further business to transact. Jack puts his money on the counter these days – I'd advise you to do the same. Now on your way, boy!'

Baffled, Ross remained where he was for a moment, searching those fleshy features for some hint of amusement. But the aging face appeared serious, wearing as always a slightly self-righteous air. For the second time in as many minutes Ross shrugged helplessly.

'If that's the way you feel about it,' he muttered.

He turned away with exaggerated carelessness and went to the door. Just as he was opening it he slipped on the worn floorboards and had to reach out a hand to steady himself.

'Watch out for my display!' Mr Hughes boomed out.

His outstretched hand groped surreptitiously along the shelf.

'Sorry about that,' he called back.

Using his body as a shield, he slid the hidden tin inside his shirt. There was no further cry of protest from Mr Hughes – only the brief whirr of the buzzer, cut off as the door swung to behind him. With a faint smile he patted the bulge in his shirt and headed for home, threading his way between the leaf-laden branches that curved low across the lane.

'All in a good cause,' he murmured as he wandered back through the hot airless afternoon.

But all at once he wasn't so sure. What the shopkeeper had said about Jack had caught him off guard. Like so many other things, it didn't make sense, yet in all honesty he couldn't bring himself to dismiss it as a joke. Somehow it stirred into life a

63

vague expectation of his own. A curious image of Jack, totally well again, returning to the village as though nothing unusual had ever occurred.

These thoughts were cut short by a loud clatter coming from the shed in his own garden. Just as he reached the back fence, his father emerged holding two dead rats. They were big animals, grey-brown, their bare tails like pieces of rubbery cord, their bloodstained mouths hanging open, revealing long incisors. He held them up for his son to see.

'There's two that won't eat the rabbits' feed,' he said.

'Don't worry,' Ross replied gloomily, 'there're plenty more to take their place.'

'True enough. Still, I suppose it stands to reason: everything else is growing like mad, so why shouldn't the vermin. It must be paradise for them, a summer like this.'

He tossed the bodies onto the compost heap and strolled towards the back door. Ross, his hand on the gate, heard himself saying, 'So you think it's reasonable, all the funny goings-on around here?'

It wasn't what he had meant to say, the question surprising even himself – he and Angie having long since agreed that there was no point in confiding in their parents. His father paused and gave him a sudden searching look.

'I've learned to take what comes,' he growled non-committally.

'But all this growth,' Ross persisted, 'and rats everywhere?'

Bill Miller scratched his neck thoughtfully. 'I've never seen anything like it, I'll grant you that,' he said in guarded tones. 'It's all a bit ...'

He squinted at the cloudless sky, searching for the right word.

'Frightening?' Ross suggested.

His father shook his head. 'Can't say it scares me. It's not what I'm used to, that's all. Makes me wonder whether the old thunderer up there's lost his grip on things.' He grinned and jerked his thumb towards the sky. 'Gone barmy, maybe, like that friend of yours, Jack.'

'There's nothing barmy about Jack,' Ross said defensively.

'Come to think of it, he has improved a bit lately. Has a different look about him.'

Ross opened the gate and walked quickly up the path. 'You're the second person to tell me that today,' he said in a tense voice.

'Well there you are, that proves it. He must have changed. Turned over a new leaf or something.'

'But how can you possibly know that?' Ross protested. 'Jack doesn't even live here any more. He left the village weeks ago.'

His father laughed and stepped into the kitchen. 'Not that I've noticed,' he called back.

TWO

Angie was waiting for him by the main gates, children jostling past her as they streamed from the school.

'What did you find out?' Ross asked.

'Hold on' – she was forced to raise her voice above the surrounding noise – 'let's get away from here first.'

They crossed the main road and turned down a side street, leaving the crowd and the noise behind. Although it was past the middle of the afternoon, the sun was still surprisingly fierce, the heat rising in waves from the pavement, the front gardens looking tired and dusty.

'Well?' he prompted her.

'I asked around and it seems he has been back. Plenty of the kids say they've seen him.'

Ross nodded reluctantly. 'It must be true then. But I still don't understand it. Why should he sneak back without telling us? That's not like him at all. It just doesn't make sense.'

'I agree,' Angie said. 'There's something funny going on.'

'Like last spring?'

'Yes, sort of.'

'Then why hasn't it affected us? We were involved last time.'

Angie ran her hand along the overgrown hedge that spilled across the low fence beside them. 'That could be because we're

66

not the ones who matter. Not really. All along it's been Jack, not us. He was the one who lost his finger, who had to run away and hide. And now it's Jack again.'

Ross considered the idea for a few moments. 'So you think someone's still after him? Trying to lure him back to the village?'

'That's one possibility.'

'Are there any others?'

She hesitated. 'I'm not sure.'

They walked on in silence for a while, Ross suddenly beginning to lag behind, glancing uneasily over his shoulder.

'What's up?' she asked.

He seemed at first not to have heard her, continuing to peer furtively back down the street.

'There's only one thing wrong with your idea,' he said at last.

'What's that?'

'We seem to be just as involved in this whole thing as Jack.'

'Why d'you say that?'

'I'll show you.'

He gave another furtive glance over his shoulder, then grasped her firmly by the arm and steered her around the corner – immediately stopping short and drawing her into the cover of the hedge.

'What are you doing?' she protested.

'You'll see in a minute.'

They waited and there was a sound of hurried footsteps, slowing down as they approached the corner. A pause, and Nigel stepped hesitantly into the open, his thin face scanning the street ahead. He spotted them only when it was too late. There was a squeal of fright and Ross had him by the scruff of the neck.

'Come on, Shrimp!' he barked out. 'What are you up to? Why are you following us?'

'I wasn't following you! Honest I wasn't!'

Ross shook him roughly. 'This is your last chance, Shrimp! The truth . . . or else!'

'All right!' he wailed.

Ross dropped him unceremoniously and gave him a light shove, sending him staggering back against the hedge.

'I'm waiting!' he said menacingly. 'And you know me! If it isn't convincing . . .'

Nigel straightened his glasses and peered anxiously along both streets.

'I had to follow you,' he said sulkily. 'It wasn't my idea.'

'What do you mean, had to?'

'Well how would you feel about going back to the hollow again? At night? And all on your own?'

'What are you talking about?'

'About the music. If I'd said no, it would have come again. But just for me this time.'

'Oh, so you admit it at last,' Ross said. 'You did hear it.'

'Yes, but I was scared that . . . you know. But then he said I'd hear it again if I didn't help him.' A look of genuine fear stole across his face, and his eyes, slightly enlarged by the round spectacles, overflowed with tears. 'I don't want to go back, Ross. Not on my own, in the dark.'

'Don't start!' Ross said warningly. 'Just tell us who put you up to this.'

'Be reasonable, Ross,' Angie interrupted. 'Can't you see he's scared?'

She put her arm around Nigel's shoulders. 'There's no reason why you have to go back to the hollow,' she said comfortingly. 'No one can make you.'

Nigel took off his glasses and dried his eyes on the cuff of his shirt. 'We had to go last time,' he said in a quavery voice.

'Yes, but that probably won't happen again. You think back to that night. At first the music called and we had to go. But later, when we got to the hollow, it didn't seem to want us. So it gave us that bad pain in the head, and after that we couldn't

68

hear it any more.'

'How d'you know it was still there?'

'It was. Ask Ross.'

'Angie's right,' Ross said. 'We weren't the only ones called to the hollow that night. There was someone else, and he had to listen to the music long after we'd stopped hearing it.'

'Couldn't it call us in a different way next time?' Nigel objected. 'Use different notes or something?'

'It's possible,' Ross admitted grudgingly, 'but we don't think it's likely. The pain we felt that night – it was like something burning out in our heads. Like . . . like a fuse blowing. A way of stopping the music getting through to us.'

'But why?'

'Because we weren't what it was after. It wanted someone else.'

'Which means we probably don't have to worry about it any more,' Angie added, trying to sound more confident than she really felt. 'What we can't hear isn't going to hurt us. That's how we see it anyway.'

'But *he* can still hurt me,' Nigel complained. 'Darned near tore my ear off the other day.'

'Your ear?'

'Yes, he was twisting it all the time he was telling me to find out where you disappear to.'

'He?' Angie asked.

Nigel edged uneasily away and Ross again grabbed him by the scruff of the neck.

'You'll get the other one twisted if you're not careful!' he threatened.

'No, please Ross!'

'Come on then! Tell us!'

'All right, but don't you let on.'

'You're the only blabbermouth around here, Shrimp.'

Nigel eyed the street mistrustfully and moved closer towards them. His voice dropped to a whisper. 'It was old Jack.'

'Are you crazy or something? It couldn't have been!'

Behind them, and close at hand, there was a faint crackling as a rat crawled through the dry litter at the base of the hedge.

'I'm telling you!' Nigel insisted. 'It was him. Jack. Straight after he got those new clothes.'

THREE

'Hello, Jack.'

He was sitting on his folded-up overcoat, his back resting against the outside wall of the shed. He opened his eyes at the sound of Angie's voice, blinking rapidly in the yellow light of late afternoon.

'Two together!' he said happily. 'Must be someone's birthday.'

He stood up as they emerged from the shadow – the sun just high enough to reach over the far lip of the valley and flood the area around the shed.

'How's the hand?' Ross asked.

'Right as rain.'

He held the now unbandaged hand up for them to see – the wound no longer angry; the fresh pink skin beginning to knit together across the blunt end of the stump, which was all that remained of his index finger.

'What do you think of that then? Stumpy, I call him, 'cause he's not a grower. Not this bit, anyway.'

Under the pretext of inspecting the wound, Ross made a quick, covert examination of Jack himself. His old, lined face was distinctly grubby; his clothes crumpled and streaked with chalk dust; his wispy grey hair grown long and tangled. There was nothing about his appearance which even faintly suggested

71

the more conventionally decent image of Jack which Mr Hughes had referred to.

'It's mending,' Ross said, releasing the hand, 'but I wouldn't go parading it in public just yet.'

'Parading it? Like in a fair? Me and the bearded lady!' He gave a throaty chuckle.

'What Ross means,' Angie explained, 'is that you shouldn't let people in the village see it. Not until it's completely healed. They might ask awkward questions.'

Jack shook his head vehemently. 'You don't catch me there! Not old Jack.'

'Haven't you been back in the past few days?' Ross asked.

Jack gave him a knowing wink. 'Not me, Ross boy. I don't fancy messing with them rats. Give you a nasty nip, they could. And I'm not up to sparing him another finger for his garden.'

He broke abruptly into song:

> *Mary, Mary, quite contrary,*
> *How does your garden grow?*

He again winked knowingly.

'How does it grow? That's the question. Well Jack's not going to find out. Let those rats creep and pry as much as they want. He won't give them a chance as well.'

Ross glanced uneasily at Angie.

'But you must have visited the village recently, Jack. Plenty of people have seen you.'

'Have they now? That's clever of them. Unless ... unless ...'

'Unless what, Jack?'

He shivered slightly, despite the warm sunlight – the sun hovering at the very rim of the valley now – and then gave himself an abrupt shake and grinned broadly.

'Unless they've got rats before the eyes. Worse than spots, 'cause they can sample your wares. Rats crawling in at your eye-sockets and out of your ears. In at your nostrils and around

72

your teeth. A tasty morsel of meat here or there.'

'Be serious, Jack,' Ross pleaded.

'Serious? Try this for size then, lad:

> *Great rats, small rats, lean rats, brawny rats,*
> *Brown rats, black rats, grey rats, tawny rats,*
> *Grave old plodders, gay young friskers,*
> > *Fathers, mothers, uncles, cousins,*
> *Cocking tails and pricking whiskers,*
> > *Families by tens and dozens.*
> *Brothers, sisters, husbands, wives –*
> *Followed the ...'*

'Jack!' Ross interrupted sharply.

He stopped and looked at them both with startled eyes, as though amazed to find he was not alone. 'Eh, what?'

'We all know about the rats, Jack,' Angie said kindly. 'It's the hot summer and bumper crops that've brought them out. They're not our reason for coming. It's you – the fact that you've been seen in the village.'

'Seen, have I? Well those aren't the eyes that matter. It's them small beady ones. Once they spy you, watch out. That nose, those whiskers, creeping through your skull and out the other side. With none of you left behind. Gone!' He snapped his fingers. 'Gone! Like that!'

Ross sighed and placed a hand gently on the old man's bony shoulder. 'Will you just answer a simple question, Jack? Have you been to the village in the past few days?'

Jack squinted up at the sun, half of which had already disappeared behind the crumbling cliff face. An uneven line of shadow was advancing rapidly across the valley floor.

'It's safer in a place like this,' he mumbled, 'away from all that growing.' He touched his wounded hand. 'Like I said, old stumpy, he won't grow again. Not him.'

'Please Jack.'

The old man gave Ross an unexpectedly level look. 'So

73

they're out hunting for me, are they? I thought it'd come to this. But don't you fret, I'll not go wandering down there, where they can pick my brains out. They're all I've got left now, my brains. He's taken all the rest.'

'Who has?'

The upper edge of the sun vanished and the encroaching shadow swallowed the rest of the valley.

'Why the rat caller. Himself, no less. The meat man, the mirror man. Old piper green.'

Ross and Angie exchanged helpless glances.

'I don't think we're getting very far,' Ross murmured, and took from his pocket the tin of spam he had stolen. 'Here, Jack, a present for you.'

He expected Jack to chuckle with pleasure, but instead he brushed it disdainfully aside.

'Brussel sprouts,' he said with strangely malicious delight, 'that'll be more my line from here on. We'll leave the likes of this to the meat man.'

'Please yourself,' Ross said, disappointed.

'That I will, lad,' he replied gleefully, 'because that way I'll be sure of not pleasing him. Spite him, it will, feeling my old gnashers chomping on his greenery.'

'Whose greenery?'

But all at once Jack seemed to lose interest in the conversation. Screwing both eyes tight shut, he began humming softly to himself, acting as if they were no longer present.

'You can be an evasive old coot when you want to,' Ross said in a disgruntled voice.

He turned away, aware that there was nothing to be got out of the old man in such a mood. In any case, it was already early dusk within the valley and he could tell from Angie's anxious expression that she was eager to leave.

'Time we were on our way then, Jack. We'll be back in a day or so. Bring you some fresh vegies. All right?'

'Aye, that'll do, that'll do.'

He waved them carelessly away, still with his eyes tight closed, rocking in time to the song he was humming.

'Goodbye, Jack.'

He made no further response, wholly intent now upon his song. As they walked back along the valley his humming followed them, gradually resolving itself into the words of a familiar jingle:

> And it seemed as if a voice,
> ... called out, 'Oh rats, rejoice!
>   The world is grown to one vast dry-saltery!
> So munch on, crunch on, take your nuncheon,
> Breakfast, supper, dinner, luncheon!'

FOUR

They stopped at the end of the lane in the early darkness. There was just enough light from the distant street to reveal the sagging outline of Jack's hut.

'I'm late enough as it is,' Angie complained.

'A few minutes won't make much difference,' Ross replied.

She hesitated briefly. 'Oh come on then.'

They approached the shadow-streaked doorway and knocked lightly. There was no answer – only a scraping sound from somewhere within the hut. Ross lifted the old-fashioned latch and pushed the door open. As they entered, a faint click, as of another door closing, reached their ears.

'What was that?' Angie asked in a nervous whisper.

'Not sure.'

Ross felt for the light switch and pushed it down. The room, as revealed by the overhead bulb, was very different from their memory of it. When they had last visited the hut, to collect some clothes for Jack, it had been tidy and, except for a fine film of dust, spotlessly clean. Now the floor was dirty and littered with half-withered leaves and grass; the bed was rumpled and unmade; and the whole interior smelled sour and unpleasant.

'Someone's been here,' Ross murmured.

'Yes, but not Jack. Surely.'

'We'll soon see.'

A low hissing sound was coming from the kitchen and they went to investigate, the dry leaves crackling beneath their feet. Here, too, there was a general air of disorder. But that wasn't all: one of the gas rings was alight, heating a frying pan half filled with brownish minced meat. More of the meat, as yet uncooked, lay heaped on the draining board. It looked several days old, greenish and slimy, and the smell made both children gag.

'Who could eat stuff like that?' Angie asked, disgusted.

'Whoever it is, he can't be far.'

They opened the back door and ventured gingerly into the overgrown garden. Straight away the grass around them rustled and shook, and long grey bodies slunk away – sinuous shapes which melted into the shadows; small beady eyes gleaming briefly before winking out; bare tails dragging between the coarse stems of grass.

'Rats!' Ross hissed.

He tried to draw Angie back into the cover of the kitchen, but she shook him off.

'Wait!'

She was looking not at the ground, but at something else – at the dark outline of a man standing only four or five paces away, his body partly shielded by the drooping branches of a willow. He remained absolutely still, as though rooted to the spot – as though he too were part of the abundant summer growth – the faint light of the distant street lamp, shining through the cascade of leaves, giving to his face and clothes a weirdly greenish hue.

'Jack,' Angie said softly, 'is that you?'

There was a pause before a familiar voice replied, 'I'm sorry, my dear. Did I startle you?'

Then, to Ross's astonishment, Jack himself parted the willow branches and stepped forward into the light spilling from the kitchen door.

'How on earth!' Ross began.

He fell silent, staggered by the transformation. Gone was the down-at-heel, threadbare appearance of the man they had left less than an hour earlier. The tangled, unruly grey hair had been cut short and combed; and the old clothes had been replaced by new. Instead of the usual baggy suit, several sizes too large, Jack was wearing a well tailored reddish-brown jacket and neatly pressed fawn-coloured trousers whose soft weave contained just a hint of yellow. Those same colours, red and yellow, were echoed in the silk tie which nestled against the spotless whiteness of his shirt.

'Well?' Jack asked, a faint smile on his lips, 'Do you approve of the change?'

'... er ... yes ... it's just that ...'

Again Ross fell silent as he felt Angie's hand tighten about his wrist.

'Would you do something for me, Jack?' she asked, a note of disarming friendliness in her voice.

'Anything at all, my dear.'

'Would you mind taking off your gloves?'

For the first time Ross noticed that he was indeed wearing cotton gloves. He saw Jack hesitate, one gloved hand clutching protectively at the other.

'Both of them?' he asked evasively.

'Yes.'

Just for a moment something gleamed in the depths of Jack's eyes: a look Ross had never expected to see there. It was gone instantly. A familiar smile spread across the worn features, followed by a low chuckle – an oddly mocking sound.

'Ah, there you have me, my dear,' he admitted.

With a few quick movements he pulled off the gloves, holding both hands up for them to see. There was no trace of a wound on the left hand, all the fingers intact.

'But I saw it happen!' Ross burst out. 'Right here, in this garden! It has to be a trick!'

'No, not a trick,' Angie answered calmly. And then to the man they had both taken for Jack: 'Who are you?'

He smiled again, slightly less pleasantly this time.

'Haven't you guessed?'

'I think so, but I want to be sure.'

'Why, Jack's other self, of course.'

'What does that mean?'

'Why, what could be clearer? I'm Jack's twin. His brother – answering to the name of Tom, by the way. Both of us born at the same hour, of the same mother, nearly seventy-three years ago.'

His face crinkled up with amusement at their shocked silence. 'I'm sorry, my dears,' he said drily, 'I seem to have startled you. That wasn't my intention. I thought you'd already guessed.'

It was Ross who found his voice first. 'Try pulling the other one,' he said scornfully, 'it's got bells on.'

'Ah, an unbeliever. A pity. And you, my dear?' – gazing at Angie.

'If what you say's true,' she said, 'why have you let people round here believe you're Jack?'

'For his own good, my pet. Dear old Jack is a little touched in the head. Not all there, as they say. Whereas I' – he indicated his own immaculate appearance – 'I thought I might improve his public image somewhat.'

'And is that the only reason you're here?'

'Not altogether. I realized he was in trouble. Twins have a way of knowing these things – a kind of instinctive sympathy. Flesh of each other's flesh and all that. So I came to take care of him.'

'You'll have to find him first,' Ross said.

'That, dear boy, is where you come in. A little help, perhaps, a few directions, all for the good of your trusted friend, naturally.'

'We haven't a clue where he is,' Angie said quickly.

The old man sniggered, his eyes shifting slyly from Ross to Angie. 'A hasty answer,' he murmured, with the faintest undertone of threat in his voice. 'I do beg of you to reconsider.'

'And if we won't?'

He bent down – this figure who was at once so like Jack and yet so alien to him – and scooped up a handful of dry grass and leaves; cradling the withered fragments in his palm and then blowing on them gently, watching with almost loving eyes as they tumbled to the ground.

'No matter,' he answered easily, 'it will come to the same thing in the end. Of that, my dear ones, I can assure you.'

FIVE

'You know how your mother carries on if you dodge school,' Ross said.

Angie was in the middle of the lane, effectively barring his way, the dry sandy earth all around them striped with shadows cast by the early morning sun.

'School!' she said scornfully. 'Is that all you can think of? After what happened last night?'

He pushed past her. 'It's better than going round in circles, puzzling over something I don't understand.'

'Oh you understand all right' – making no effort to veil the sarcasm in her voice.

He turned to face her, the sun, still low in the sky, shining straight into his eyes, dazzling him. 'If you're referring to the old man,' he said defensively, 'then I agree with you. He isn't Jack's brother, whatever he may say. But so what? Where does that get us?'

'You know more than that, Ross. Be honest.'

'Do I?'

He glanced at his watch and began walking slowly along the lane. He thought for a moment she had relented and was following. That was partly why she caught him by surprise.

'Clone!' – the word nearly shouted at him.

He faltered, stopping and slewing round in a single move-

81

ment. 'What?'

'You heard me.'

'You've been reading too many books, Angie, d'you know that?'

'Perhaps you haven't read enough.'

He came back to where she was standing. 'Enough to realize what clone means. A complete living creature grown from tissue taken from another creature. A perfect carbon copy of the original.'

'Well?'

'But that's ridiculous! He couldn't be!'

'Why not?'

'Because it all sounds too far-fetched.'

'D'you have a better explanation?'

'There must be one.'

'Must there? You said yourself he isn't Jack's brother. So where does that leave us?'

'But a clone!'

'It's the only reasonable explanation, Ross. Think about it. Jack's put into a trance and made to chop off his finger. Still in a trance, he takes the finger into the woods, presumably to someone waiting for him in the hollow.'

'Why the hollow?'

'Because Jack went back there and attacked the place with an axe. He sensed that something was hiding there, the thing that had been controlling him. Anyway, after that no trace of the finger is found. Then months later a perfect copy of Jack appears, but with ten fingers instead of nine, which is exactly what you'd expect.'

'Not quite a perfect copy,' Ross said quietly.

'How's he different?'

'He hasn't got Jack's mind. He's not the same inside.'

'Yes, I suppose that's true,' Angie conceded. 'But a perfect copy in every other way. You can't deny that.'

Ross nodded, though with obvious reluctance.

'All right, but are we really any wiser? Why should anyone want to make a copy of Jack?'

Angie gave him an almost accusing look. 'That's what I want you to help me find out. But it seems you'd rather stick your head in the sand like Nigel.'

He winced. 'Was I beginning to sound that bad?'

'Nearly.'

He grinned ruefully at her. 'That doesn't leave me much choice, does it?'

SIX

'I'm not sure why it is,' Ross said uneasily, 'but this place gives me a funny feeling.'

He and Angie had stopped at the lip of the hollow and were gazing down.

'You said it worried you once before,' Angie reminded him.

'I know. I can't help feeling there's something wrong here.'

'Such as what?'

'The trees maybe,' he said hesitantly. 'The two big ones. It could be something to do with them.'

'Let's take a closer look, then.'

They made their way down the slope towards the pine tree.

The axe wounds were still visible, as was the black scorch mark which ran the length of the trunk.

'What about that?' Angie asked, pointing to the scorch mark.

'I suppose it is a bit odd. Wonder how it happened?'

'Lightning perhaps. That or . . .'

'Or what?'

'Don't laugh,' she said, 'it's only a suggestion – but d'you remember that evening we were all out in the garden and something fell from the sky? Nigel called it a comet. Well that might have caused it.'

Ross went closer to the tree and inspected the ground at its base.

'That's not such a silly idea,' he said at last. 'Look at this. Something could easily have landed here.'

He indicated a shallow depression, barely visible, about two or three paces across and roughly circular in shape. Within the circle, the grass was thinner than elsewhere, as though more recently sown.

'It certainly looks suspicious,' Angie said. 'And it wasn't long after the comet or whatever it was that we first heard the music.'

At the mention of the word music, Ross stood up and looked uneasily around him. 'This bit of ground probably has something to do with what's going on here. But right now it isn't what's getting to me. There's something else. More obvious. Ordinary even.'

He walked over to the elm tree and stopped beneath its spreading boughs, gazing up into the dense foliage.

'Not much to see here,' he murmured. 'It's too thick. You'd need a torch. Though maybe if I climbed up.'

He jumped for the lowest bough, grasped it with both hands, and was just hoisting himself up when a faint snatch of music drifted down towards him – not from the tree, but from further up the slope. Instantly he dropped to the ground and gazed in the direction of the sound. There, at the top of the rise, was Jack's double, the old man who called himself Tom. He was blowing softly on some kind of pipe, though he took it from his lips as soon as he had attracted their attention.

'Good day, my dears,' he called out.

With surprising agility, he ran lightly down the slope, picking his way expertly between the bushes and young trees, as though he had followed such a route many times before.

'Are you spying on us?' Angie asked accusingly.

He smiled at them in a friendly way. Then, reaching up, he brushed his hand gently against the foliage of the elm tree,

85

caressing the clusters of leaves much as he might have done a dog or cat.

'Beautiful, isn't it?' he said admiringly. He swept his arm round in a half circle, including in his gesture the whole of the surrounding woodland. 'All of it,' he sighed, 'so beautiful. Not like other things I could mention.'

He turned his eyes to Angie and Ross, and at once the contented smile left his face.

'Not like us, you mean?' Ross asked.

'That is a way of putting it,' he assented vaguely.

'How else would you put it?' Angie asked him.

He fingered the curiously shaped musical instrument he was holding. In general appearance it closely resembled the pipes of Pan.

'Surely, my pet,' he said, his voice noticeably harsher, 'you would not compare yourself with a tree!'

'Why not?' She tried to sound airy, unconcerned. 'Human beings and trees are both living things.'

He reached up and again caressed the elm leaves. 'But consider a tree in its wholeness,' he said, 'its perfection of form, its grace, its variety of texture. It is nothing less than a masterpiece. Even in decay it remains wholesome, sweet. Whereas you and your friend here are but *flesh*!' He almost spat the word at them. 'Corruptible flesh, fit only to nourish the earth.'

He plucked disdainfully at the wrinkled skin of his own hand.

'He seems to be referring to those heaps of meat rotting in his kitchen,' Ross said sarcastically.

'Or to Jack's body,' Angie added quietly, 'which he now wears.'

The old man's eyes glittered dangerously. 'Ah, I see my two dear ones are very clever. Let me congratulate you. You reason most effectively. I wonder, though, how well you dance.'

Lifting the pipes to his lips, he blew softly upon them and a strange haunting refrain swelled out into the woodland. The sound of the pipes themselves was not familiar, but the melody, its sinuous, elusive quality, was identical to that which had enticed them to this spot months before, and straight away Ross and Angie stiffened with apprehension. The first notes were like a cascade of raindrops, a cool shower falling through sunlight. Thereafter they evoked an image of living greenery, of probing tendrils which endlessly criss-crossed and interlaced, forming a complex pattern, a net of sound that strove to enmesh everything it touched. For several minutes the music rose and fell in subtle modulations, weaving itself about the listening children in what was obviously intended as a binding spell. But on this occasion it failed to ensnare them.

'You're wasting your time, you know,' Ross said loudly, trying to hide his relief at finding he was immune to the music's power.

The music stopped abruptly. With a look of ill-concealed malice, Tom slipped the pipes into his jacket pocket.

'You didn't plan things very well, did you?' Angie said, and laughed. 'You should have foreseen this months ago, when you rejected us and chose Jack instead. That pain in our heads – it cured us of your music for ever.'

Tom smiled bitterly. 'That, my dear young creature, was an oversight. I freely admit it. As was the disappearance of our good friend and brother, Jack. But they are small errors and shall be duly rectified. In the meantime I must crave your patience.'

He made an elaborate, ironic bow.

'Why should we be patient?' Ross asked. 'What's to stop us letting everyone in the village know what's going on?'

'Your own good sense, dear boy. Believe me, I am experienced in these matters. Who would take your wild accusations seriously? They'd class you with poor dispensable Jack. Another head-case, they'd say.'

'Well don't expect us just to sit around and do nothing,' Ross retorted. 'We have our own plans.'

'And such plans!' Tom's tone was now far more mocking and

assured. 'Searching this hollow, for instance! Why, what did you expect to find? Did you think these innocent trees would whisper secrets to you? That the leaves and grass would lay bare their hearts?' He clicked his tongue disapprovingly. 'Really, my dears, I'm surprised at you. Surely you realize – what is the quaint expression? – that the die is now cast.'

'What are you getting at?' Angie asked.

He pointed to himself. 'As you see, I have already arrived.'

'You mean it's too late to do anything here?'

'I deeply regret, for your sakes of course, that such is the case.'

'We'll see about that!' Ross said. But the threat sounded empty even to his own ears. He added lamely, 'Come on, Angie, let's leave him to his precious trees and grass.'

Resisting the temptation to hurry, they walked up the slope, pausing briefly at the top to look back.

Tom was sitting between the two giant trees, rather like a sentry set to guard some invisible treasure.

'What do you make of him?' Ross murmured.

'Wrong question,' Angie answered shortly. 'There's no "him". Only an "it". It.'

SEVEN

Ross, gazing through the window of the headmaster's study, noticed the clothing first of all. It was unmistakable, the reddish-brown jacket and yellowish trousers almost garish in the drab street. He edged away from the desk, hoping for a slightly better view, while in the background the headmaster's voice droned on.

'It's the kind of thing I've come to expect from you, Miller, but I had hoped that in your case, Angie ...'

'It wasn't Ross's fault, Sir. It was really my idea.'

Ross, only half listening, watched as the familiar figure raised both arms, as though pleading with the circle of listeners.

'I'm sorry to hear that,' the headmaster went on. 'I expected more of you, young woman, especially after the warning I gave the pair of you last time.'

A pause, in which Ross noticed Nigel join the onlookers.

'Very well, that's all for the time being. You do realize, of course, that I'll be contacting your parents.'

'Yes, Sir.'

'Miller!'

Suddenly aware that he was being addresseed, Ross glanced round quickly. '... er ... yes, Sir.'

In silence, he followed Angie out into the corridor.

'What were you dreaming about in there?' she asked as soon as the door had closed behind them.

'It's Tom, he's here, outside.'

'Waiting for us?'

'I'm not sure. There's a crowd of kids round him.'

They reached the main exit and peered out. Tom was standing on the pavement just beyond the school gates, addressing a circle of children. Even though his voice failed to carry as far as the school building, it was clear from his gestures that he was speaking with some passion.

Angie and Ross left the building and stole unobtrusively across the playground. As they drew closer, Tom's words reached them in snatches, fragments of sentences tossed about by the warm afternoon breeze.

'... not here ... no place here, but out there ... freedom of natural growth ... living world of the countryside, where those who ... unblemished by cars and so-called human developments ... all who really seek peace ... amidst the unspoilt beauty of ...'

Ross, leading the way, sidled through the main gates and up to Nigel who was standing at the edge of the pavement.

'What's he going on about?' he asked Nigel in a whisper.

'He's off his head. Listen to him.'

Tom, an unctuous smile on his lips, gazed fondly at his audience. 'Let me lead you away from this noise and chaos,' he continued, 'away from the imprisonment of roads and houses and schools, to a place of seclusion.'

'He wants us to join him in the mad house!' a boy called out.

There was a burst of laughter, and Ross and Angie suddenly realized that the crowd had gathered there only to make fun of the old man.

'I do entreat you all ...' He tried vainly to make himself heard.

'Thinks he's John the Baptist!' someone else yelled.

'And everyone knows what happened to him!'

'Looks to me more like a scarecrow in that jacket and trousers. Old Worzel come to take us for a picnic!'

'Yes, he had a replaceable head, too!'

Soon the individual cat-calls were indistinguishable, lost in the general clamour. Laughing and shouting, the crowd began to press forward, the circle gradually narrowing. Yet Tom, despite the jostling, continued to smile benevolently. He actually seemed to be enjoying the situation, as though this was what he had hoped for all along.

Angie, watching from the sidelines, leaned towards Ross. 'What's he up to?'

'I don't know. But at this rate someone's going to get hurt.'

Ross, who was older than most of the children present, began forcing his way through the crowd. But long before he could reach the centre of the circle, Tom took the pipes from his pocket and raised them quickly, almost slyly to his lips. At the very first note, all the noise and pushing stopped. One moment Ross was struggling through an unruly mob; the next he was standing amongst a group of silent, oddly listless children. As the melody enveloped them, their faces lost all expression: they stood with mouths open, gazing into space.

'Stop him!' Angie called out.

Ross reached across the heads of those barring his way and tried to grab at the reddish-brown jacket. But Tom merely stepped out of reach, the crowd surging after him. Ross lunged again, with the same result, the crowd hemming him in now, their mask-like faces turned obediently towards the lilting melody.

'Angie!' Ross called out.

She also began to struggle through the crowd, her hands stretched out towards him. Before their fingers could touch, the music died away, and immediately an utter stillness settled upon the afternoon – a few seconds of shocked silence which even the rumble of a passing lorry somehow failed to shatter.

'Yes, very satisfactory,' Tom murmured.

He clicked his fingers once, twice, and slowly the faces of those gathered about him began to regain the warmth and animation they had lost. Eyes no longer sightless registered bewilderment, as though astonished by the everyday appearance of street and school. Some of the smaller children half covered their faces in alarm, stepping back from the old man who stood amongst them.

'Home now, dear ones,' he said softly, waving his hands.

They were too shaken and confused to protest. A few hesitated, glancing at each other fearfully. But they did not delay for long, and soon they too were hurrying down the street with lowered eyes. Only Angie and Ross remained, with Nigel cowering uncertainly behind them.

'Quite impressive,' Ross said sarcastically, having to struggle to keep his voice steady. 'But what's it all for?'

Tom turned his cold eyes upon him. 'Let us call it a trial run, dear boy.'

'For what?'

'For what is to come. But not yet. Everything, as we say, in its season.'

Pocketing the pipes, he walked away. Nigel, directly in his path and too shocked to move, was pushed roughly aside – his glasses, dislodged by the jolt, tumbling to the ground. Momentarily the twin lenses caught the sunlight, and then Tom brought his foot down on them, snapping the frames across the bridge.

'I can't see!' Nigel wailed, scrabbling in the gutter.

Tom glanced back. 'Nor are you meant to, my dear,' he said.

Angie was already helping Nigel to his feet. 'We may not be as blind as you think!' she said angrily.

'And what have you seen, my special pet?'

'I've just realized who you are. Or at least the kind of role you're playing.'

His hand moved instinctively towards the pocket which held

the pipes. He checked the gesture just in time. 'Do tell me your little secret, sweet one,' he said with forced friendliness.

'It was something Jack mentioned. An old poem about rats.'

'Our dear brother Jack,' he broke out impatiently, 'has an overripe imagination. One day I shall pluck it from him.'

With that parting threat, he strode off down the street.

'What's going on?' Nigel whined, still clinging to Angie. 'What have rats got to do with us? Or him?'

Angie didn't answer, looking instead at Ross. He stared back at her.

'Everything,' he replied soberly.

EIGHT

It was the sharp pain which woke him. He sat up in bed, his hand clamped instinctively to the side of his neck. Even in those first dazed moments of consciousness he realized he had been bitten: he could feel the small wound with the tips of his fingers, a shallow depression where a sliver of skin had been neatly sliced away; and when he spread his hand in the moonlight he could see the mauve-coloured smear of blood staining his palm.

Seconds later he realized something else: that he was not alone in the room. Whatever had wounded him was still there, hiding in the shadows. He reached for the bedside lamp and clicked it on. It cast a small pool of brightness, the heavy shade containing most of the light and spilling it onto his pillow. Yet enough escaped into the far corners of the room to reveal what he was after: two beady eyes, unwinking; and behind them the long grey-furred body terminating in a naked rope of tail.

Ross rolled off the bed, gathering one of his shoes as he did so, and stood up on the cool lino. The rat had not moved, its tiny eyes fixed on him, only its whiskers twitching slightly. Shoe in hand, Ross edged around the bed, putting himself between the animal and the half-open window. Slowly he drew the shoe back and up, ready to strike.

In a single fluid movement the rat slid along the wall and up onto the bed, stopping just out of range, its long sinuous body draped across the brightly lit pillow. From that position it had an open run to the window: a few swift bounds, a leap from the bed end, and it would be gone. But it showed no inclination to escape, its body tensed and still, as though waiting.

Ross advanced again – and again it moved beyond his reach, its body making a faint plopping sound as it dropped to the floor and slid into the far corner. Never once did it take its eyes from him, the head turned always in his direction, so that when he threw the shoe the animal easily dodged aside – running straight up the side of the chest-of-drawers and taking refuge behind the silver-mounted photograph of his mother.

'What's going on in there?' – his father's voice, thick with sleep, from the neighbouring room.

'Nothing, Dad.'

He retrieved the shoe and stood watching the rat, allowing the drowsy silence to settle upon the house once more. And it was then, during those suspended moments, that he detected it: a vibrant feeling in the air that grew stronger as the seconds passed; a steady wave-like pulsation that made his flesh tingle and his hair stir at the back of his neck. Nor was that all: intertwined with it, like the tendrils of a dependent vine lacing themselves about an existing stem, was a distinct sound, an actual strain of music. Not the melody he had heard before. Different, yet no less melodic, more high-pitched and reedy. Played, unmistakably, on Tom's pipes.

As it drew nearer the rat's nose twitched with anticipation. Its eyes remained fixed upon Ross, but its body had half turned, its back legs drawn in, spring-like, beneath it. Too late, Ross guessed what was happening. The pipes were already in the lane, passing his own back fence, and as he leaped forward, the rat dropped rapidly to the floor. He swung wildly as it scampered past him, missing it by a wide margin and slipping dangerously on the worn lino. By the time he had regained his balance the rat was already out of the window and slithering down the slate roof.

He lost sight of it after that. But he saw Tom clearly enough, walking along the moonlit lane blowing softly on his pipes. And behind him, like a sinister living stream, came the massed bodies of the rats. There was more than a score of them, close-packed, loping along at his heels.

Ross had already begun pulling on his clothes – pausing only long enough to knock twice, softly, on the connecting wall. There was an answering knock, and less than a minute later Angie joined him outside, the two of them crouched on the kitchen roof.

'You were right,' he whispered, 'he's leading them away, the same as in the poem.'

'Not exactly the same,' Angie replied. 'There's one difference.'

'What's that?'

'These.'

She pointed to the wound on Ross's neck, then turned her head sideways, revealing a similar mark just below her ear.

'So they got you too,' Ross said. 'But why have them bite us? What's the point?'

'Can't you guess?' she answered darkly.

Ross fingered the still weeping wound and shivered slightly.

'Well?' Angie pressed him.

'I'm tired of guessing,' he said. 'This time I want to be sure.'

NINE

They caught a glimpse of him over near the trees, his wispy hair showing silver in the moonlight, the grass behind him agitated by the passage of the rats. He had disappeared long before they could cross the field, the pipe music scarcely audible now, filtering faintly through the dense barrier of leaves and branches. Yet they didn't falter. There was only one path through the thick undergrowth – the one leading to the hollow – and they quickly located it and entered the warm darkness of the wood.

Soon the sound of the pipes was clearer, less fitful, the strangely high-pitched melody swelling out around them. It grew louder as they advanced, and for the first time since setting out they slowed down. Immediately ahead lay the rim of the hollow, and with extreme caution they left the cover of the trees and stepped out into the open. There below them, still with the mass of grey bodies at his heels, was Tom.

'We've got him!' Angie whispered excitedly.

But she had spoken too soon. Instead of stopping beneath the two giant trees, as they had expected, Tom led the rats up the other side of the hollow and back into the woods.

'What the devil's he up to?' Ross murmured.

They also crossed the hollow, found the path Tom had taken, and set off in pursuit. For some time they had no idea where they were being led – blundering through the darkness, guided only by the feel of the path beneath their feet and the high wavering melody. Then, very gradually, the ground began to slope downwards.

'The river!' Ross said in an excited whisper. 'He's headed for the river! Exactly like the story!'

'But surely he's not going to drown them,' Angie answered.

'Why not?'

'You know why. Because he isn't really...'

Ross stopped suddenly and Angie cannoned into him.

'What's the matter?'

'The caves!' he said. 'On the other side of the river. Aren't they also part of the story?'

'The poem describes an opening in a hill, but that comes later.'

'I don't care when it comes. That's where he's taking them. To the caves.'

'Yes, you could be right.'

'Which means it's no good trailing after him. Without a light we can't possibly follow him underground. We have to cut him off – stop him before he gets there.'

Leaving the path, he began forcing his way through the ferns and bushes that grew thickly beneath the trees. It was hard going at first, but as they plunged deeper into the valley the ground became more rocky and the undergrowth thinned out. Without the tangle of fern and bramble to impede them, they were soon running between the trees, picking out a zig-zag path which enabled them to skirt the sound of the music and reach the bottom of the slope minutes ahead of Tom.

They stopped on the banks of the river and looked about them. The moon was high and they could see quite clearly. On the opposite bank, showing as a half circle of darkness, was the entrance to the labyrinth of caves that honeycombed the hillside. There was no bridge across the river, but further upstream could be seen the eroded remains of a causeway – fragments of shattered rock that now served as stepping stones.

'That's the place to stop him,' Angie said.

They ran upstream and stood waiting on a stretch of shingle bank, the stepping stones behind them. From the darkness came the sound of the pipes. The melody floated down, increasing in volume and filling the night with a weird sense of disquiet. The source of that melody was so close now that Angie and Ross could hear, beneath the piping, the rustle of footsteps and a chorus of tiny high-pitched squeaks. There was a flicker of movement at the very edge of the trees, and all at once the music rose to a crescendo and stopped.

'Ah, a reception committee' – Tom's voice issuing from the silence and the darkness.

A moment later he stepped out into the open, the rats, squeaking in agitation, milling about his feet.

'Have my dear friends come to wish me well?' he asked mockingly.

'We're here to stop you,' Ross said in level tones.

'A very laudable enterprise, dear boy. But doomed, I fear, to failure'

'Why?'

'Need you ask?'

Tom lifted the pipes to his lips and blew a series of oddly discordant notes. Immediately the rats formed themselves into a phalanx of threatening grey bodies.

'No!' Angie shouted.

The line surged forward. There was a flash of sharp white teeth, a gleam of tiny menacing eyes, an overpowering smell of rodent, strong and pungent. And then, thankfully, Tom lowered the pipes.

'You see,' he said, 'there is no question of your preventing me.'

Somewhere in the woods an owl hooted, a peculiarly friendly sound within that eery setting. The rats, although no longer advancing, held their threatening pose, their eyes silver-black,

99

gleaming dangerously.

'Come on, Ross,' Angie urged him, tugging at his sleeve.

He didn't argue, both of them moving aside, leaving the causeway clear.

Tom nodded approvingly. 'Allow me to say, dear children, that you have made a most fortunate choice. It would not have been wise to try and bargain, let us say, with my small companions. Not in their present mood.'

Angie was about to make an angry reply, but Ross gripped her hand and shook his head. Tom, turning contemptuously away, did not even notice the gesture. He was again blowing on his pipes, softly, enticingly, the rats tumbling over each other in their eagerness to crowd in behind him. With slow deliberate steps, he walked down the shingle bank and began jumping lightly from one ledge of rock to the next. The rats, as before, followed his every move, their plump, well-fed bodies slithering across the damp stepping-stones.

A few more leaps and they would all have been across. Tom was already clambering up towards the black mouth of the cave, most of the rats dragging their long naked tails through the shallows on the far bank. Only a handful of them remained in the centre of the river, huddled together, momentarily isolated as they waited their turn to jump onto the smallest and most precarious of the stepping-stones.

That was when Ross acted. Scrabbling in the shingle at his feet, he gathered a handful of pebbles and threw three of them in quick succession at the mass of tightly wedged bodies. The first two overshot their mark, but the third clipped a rat on the side of the head and sent it tumbling into the river.

'Quick! Grab hold of it!' he yelled.

Angie ran downstream, snatched up a length of half-rotten stick, and reached as far as she could out into the river. In the moonlight the water was black and opaque, and it was more by luck than judgement that she made contact with the silent grey form as it drifted past. It lodged against the very end of the stick, swung slowly out of the current, and floated in towards the shore. Ross, kneeling beside her, scooped it out of the shallows with both hands, the heavy body now lifeless and still.

'Got it!' he said, holding it up triumphantly.

Through the arch of his own raised arms he saw Tom staring balefully at him from the far bank.

'You will pay for that, dear boy,' he said, his voice suddenly as cold as his eyes. 'Oh, not immediately. Later. When the time is ripe. Yes, ripe, that is the appropriate word. And on that occasion there will be no mistake, as there was with our dear brother Jack. You yourself will see to that.'

'Me?'

'Yes, you, foolish child.'

He chuckled mirthlessly and turned away. Piping softly, he clambered up the hillside and disappeared into the cave, the rats close behind him – the music growing rapidly fainter, finally fading into nothing.

'What did he mean, that you'd see there was no mistake?' Angie asked.

'Never mind about that now,' Ross said impatiently.

He was already feeling in his pocket for his penknife. He pulled out the main blade and laid the rat down on the bank, belly up.

'Do you have to slit it open?' Angie asked.

'How else can we find out?'

The blade was poised above the slack fur of the abdomen.

'You could try the mouth first.'

He put the knife down and eased the slack jaws apart. There was something just behind the bottom incisors – something grey-white and soft. He lifted it out with the tip of his finger. Even in the moonlight they could see it was a tiny sliver of human flesh.

TEN

Jack took it delicately between finger and thumb and held it up to the sunlight. In the harsh brightness of early morning it could almost have been mistaken for a scrap of paper.

'What do you make of it?' Angie asked.

He gave it back to Ross and wiped his fingers. 'Aye, that's his handiwork,' he muttered. 'Up to his tricks again.'

'What tricks?' Ross prompted him.

'Why that's a grower, isn't it?' He indicated the sliver of flesh. 'A grower. Same as he took from me. My old pointer that he stole' – rubbing, as he spoke, at the stump of his severed finger.

'But why is he doing this?'

'I told you, didn't I. Weeks back. A dealer in meat, that's him.'

'In human meat?'

'Nothing but the best. He decided that early on. Killed the birds, he did, without so much as a by-your-leave. Not good enough for him, they weren't, not for his lordship. So he let them fall.'

Ross suppressed an impatient sigh. 'We know about that, Jack,' he said, 'but it doesn't help us much. We have to find out what's behind it all. Who he is.'

The old man placed a cautionary finger on his lips and beck-oned for them both to follow him into the dusty interior of the hut. 'He's not the only one,' he whispered secretively. 'It's not just old piper Tom, not by a long chalk. He's just the delivery boy, moving his fingers on the pipes, that's all.'

'Who else is there?'

Jack drew them closer still, an arm around each of their shoulders – his watery eyes jerking nervously towards the window. 'There's him as calls the tune. The green one. A piece of starfall hiding out there in the woods. He's the one. Always.'

Clearing his throat, he began to sing softly:

> Boys and girls come out to play,
> The moon doth shine as bright as day,
> Leave your supper and leave your sleep
> And join your playfellows in the street.

Angie waited for him to finish. 'Do you know where he's hidden, Jack?'

'Not I. But he's out there. Didn't I hear him when he called for the old pointer? Didn't I take it to him?'

'And this is the person you call the meat dealer?'

Jack wagged his head at them reprovingly. 'I didn't say nothing about a person.'

The one who's caused the trouble then, who sent the piper?'

Jack screwed up one eye and gave them a knowing look. 'Growers.' He pronounced the word slowly, significantly. 'That's what he's after.'

He winked at them and again broke into song:

> Mary, Mary, quite contrary,
> How does your garden grow?
> With silver bells and cockle shells
> And pretty maids all in a row.

He paused and took a deep breath. 'Pretty maids,' he added, 'that'll be half of them.'

'All right, Jack,' Angie agreed, 'more growers, like his piper.

103

But what for? Why does he need them?'

'Ah, that'd be telling.'

'Can't you tell us?'

Jack suddenly dropped his conspiratorial air and gazed forlornly at his damaged hand. 'He's a devil for secrets, that one,' he murmured. 'Hid away, he did, when I took the axe to him. A song for a song, I says, 'cause that's fair. And then I sang it out loud, *"Here comes a chopper to chop off your head."* Yours this time, meat man. But he hid.'

'So you don't know what he's really up to, Jack?'

'No, but I'll tell you this: he has no more use for me. Nor for you two pretty soon. That's why I've been cleaning out the corners. For when the three of us are living here. Us and the axe together. Cosy like.'

He reached out and touched the axe which lay on the windowsill beside the bed, running his hand trustingly over the heavy metal head.

Angie glanced across at Ross, trying to mask her disappointment.

'We're not getting very far,' she said ruefully. 'It's like last night, except now there are three of us floundering in the dark.'

Ross went to the open door and gazed across at the opposite side of the valley. The chalk cliff-face showed as a flat expanse of creamy whiteness in the brilliant sunlight.

'We don't have to remain in the dark if we don't want to,' he said.

'What are you suggesting?'

'We could go to the caves now. Have a look for ourselves.'

'But you said they go a really long way back into the hillside. We could search forever. In any case, I wouldn't fancy facing those rats again, not on our own.'

Ross turned towards her. 'That's just it, we needn't be alone. Last night, when he was calling the rats, he must have woken other people in the village. They would have seen him too and

104

realized something's going on.'

Angie shook her head. 'Not necessarily. Apart from Nigel, we're the only ones not affected by the music. The others probably stayed asleep. How else can you explain why nobody but us followed him? Why nobody screamed out when they were bitten?'

Jack chuckled quietly to himself in the corner, gently waggling the stump of his missing finger.

'All right,' Ross conceded, 'so they all stayed asleep. That doesn't stop us telling someone now. We can't go on keeping this to ourselves.'

'Who do you propose we confide in?'

'Our parents, someone at school . . .'

'Oh great!' Angie broke in. 'I can just picture it, the two of us trying to convince my mother that some mysterious piper character has stepped out of a fairy story and invaded the village! She'll think we're crazy. And so would anyone else.'

'So what do we do?' he said.

'Have you got any other ideas?'

'No.'

'Then I suppose we'll just have to wait.'

'For what?'

Jack, watching them from the corner, again let out a low chuckle and began to chant softly to himself:

> *There was a rustling that seemed like a bustling,*
> *Of merry crowds justling at pitching and hustling,*
> *Small feet were pattering, wooden shoes clattering,*
> *Little hands clapping and little tongues chattering,*
> *And, like fowls in a farm-yard when barley is scattering,*
> *Out came the children running.*

PART III
AUTUMN

ONE

'You've got to hand it to him,' Bill Miller said, 'he's not the layabout he used to be. Though if you ask me he's still a bit cracked.'

'Maybe,' Ross answered vaguely.

He was gazing out of the living-room window, not really listening. After months of patient watchfulness, of being constantly on the lookout for a telltale sign, he had lost that first edge of alertness. And now, confronted at last by the clue he had been waiting for, he nearly failed to recognize it.

'Take this latest scheme of his,' Bill Miller continued. 'Says he's reviving an old tradition. An autumn festival, he calls it. The way it used to be, with flute playing and kids dancing around to welcome in the new season. Well, I suppose it doesn't do any harm, but ...'

Ross stood up abruptly. 'Did you say flute playing?'

'Something like that. A country romp to keep the kids off the streets.'

'When?'

'Today, as far as I remember. I thought you might ...'

But Ross didn't hear the rest – already running through the kitchen, slamming the door behind him.

He paused for a few moments on the back step, listening. It was a cool autumn day, damp and still, yellowing leaves drifting lazily from the trees. He held his breath, straining to pick up the faintest, most distant noises. But apart from the intermittent traffic on the road and the sound of someone humming softly to himself near by, nothing disturbed the silence.

He peered over the side fence and saw Mr Bowles kneeling beside a row of his beloved chrysanthemums.

'Angie about?' he asked.

Mr Bowles stood up, his balding head pink from the effort of bending over.

'I'd leave her alone if I were you, lad,' he said, not unkindly. 'You know what the wife thinks of you two spending time together.'

'I only want to ask her something, Mr Bowles. Honest.'

'Well right now she's at the shop with her mum.'

'Thanks, Mr Bowles.'

He vaulted over the back fence and ran down the lane, his footsteps muffled by the carpet of soggy leaves. Still at a half run, he burst into the shop, the buzzer whirring above his head.

'Have a care, you young hooligan!' Mr Hughes said angrily.

'Sorry, Mr Hughes.'

'It's not words of apology we want,' Mrs Bowles said unpleasantly, 'it's more gentlemanly behaviour. Still' – she gave a long-suffering sigh – 'what can you expect from a home like that.'

Ross bit back an angry reply and sauntered up beside Angie who gave him an apologetic look.

'Mrs B's got a point there,' the shopkeeper added, waving a thick index finger under Ross's nose. 'When it comes to gentlemanly behaviour, even Jack could teach you a thing or two. I'd go as far as to call him a credit to the lane.'

'It was Jack I came to ask about,' Ross put in quickly.

'Glad to hear it.'

'Dad mentioned something about him taking the local kids off to celebrate the autumn festival.'

The shopkeeper nodded. 'So he has.'

'Has?'

'Yes, half an hour back. Came past here playing that flute of his with twenty or more kids in tow. Having a right old time by the looks of things. I'm sorry you weren't amongst them. Bit of innocent fun like that'd do you good.'

Ross was aware of Angie already edging towards the door. 'Do you know where they were going?' he asked.

Mr Hughes waved a fleshy hand in the direction of the lane and field. 'Oh, over there somewhere. The woods, I daresay.'

The buzzer whirred as Angie wrenched the door open. Mrs Bowles whirled around. 'Where are you off to, my girl?'

Angie didn't answer, looking straight at Ross. 'What are you standing there for?' she said impatiently. 'Didn't you hear him?'

'But half an hour!'

'There may still be time!'

He moved to the nearest bank of shelves and grabbed a plastic torch and a pack of batteries. 'Put these on the slate, will you, Mr Hughes?' he called as he crossed to the door.

'Hey! What the devil!'

'Angie!' Mrs Bowles wailed.

The door swung closed on their protest, Angie the first one across the lane, climbing rapidly over the paling fence which bordered the field. Ross crammed the torch and batteries into his pocket and scrambled after her. As he dropped down into the damp grass there was a thud of footsteps in the lane and Nigel's thin face appeared at the top of the palings.

'Where you going, Ross?'

'It's Tom, leading some kids off to the woods. You'd better come along.'

Nigel backed hurriedly away from the fence. 'I'd like to, Ross, really, but Mum won't let me.'

'Never mind about that. You know what happens when he plays his flute. They'll be needing help.'

'But I can't come! She'll kill me if I nick off!'

111

'Ross!' Angie called. 'We're wasting time!'

'Please yourself then, Shrimp. But you'll probably regret it. You might need some help yourself pretty soon.'

He turned and followed Angie across the field, heading straight for the slight gap in the trees where the path began. There was no need for them to work out a plan of action: they both knew what had to be done. Alternately running and walking, they wound their way through the woods in the direction of the hollow. It was deserted when they reached it, the giant trees, the elm and the pine, standing straight and still in the grey autumn air. They crossed to the other side, passing between the two trees – Ross, as always, experiencing a strange feeling of unease as he did so. But he said nothing, aware that they had no time to lose, that if they didn't hear the strains of the flute soon, there would be no point in going on.

The first distant notes reached them as they began the long descent into the valley – a faint suggestion of melody drifting up through the yellowing autumn leaves.

'Listen!' Ross whispered.

He paused, his head turned to one side. Angie was breathing heavily, her cheeks flushed with exertion.

'That's it!' she said.

They began running again, gathering speed as they plunged deeper into the valley. The notes of the flute were clear and strong now, coming from only a short distance ahead. But the river too was not far off: swollen from the recent days of rain, it provided a dull background murmur which grew steadily louder. Above the noise of both river and flute, childlike cries, sharp and joyful, filtered through the trees.

'They're nearly there!' Angie gasped out.

She, like Ross, was staggering with fatigue, running with her head thrown back, her mouth open as she sucked in the cool damp air. Yet they somehow managed to quicken their pace, leaping recklessly down the steepest, rockiest section of the path. The edge of the woods rushed to meet them, a yellow-green veil of leaves brushed hastily aside as they burst out onto the river bank.

They were, as they both saw at a glance, perhaps a minute too late. Tom had already reached the far bank: still playing on his flute, he was ushering the crowd of laughing, excited children across the eroded causeway. His cold eyes, as he played, swivelled round and rested momentarily on Ross and Angie, then flicked indifferently away.

'Stop him!' Angie cried in a hoarse whisper.

But she knew as well as Ross that for the moment at least they were helpless. The first of the children – all of whom they knew from school, so many familiar friendly faces – had begun to clamber up the opposite bank. Even the smaller, slower ones had passed the midpoint of the stream, leaping hazardously from rock to rock, the dark brown water, heavy with silt, swirling about their feet. They gained the far shore, making eagerly for the mouth of the cave. Only Tom remained at the water's edge, like a sentry standing guard over the crossing. He glanced behind him only once, to ensure that all was well with his charges, and then he too began to ascend the bank, walking slowly backwards, his eyes glittering dangerously, as though in warning, his fingers moving rapidly over the stops of the flute.

'What can we do?' Angie said desperately.

Ross's answer was to reach into his pocket. It took him only a few moments to tear the plastic wrapping from the batteries and fit them into the cheap plastic torch. Then, having flicked the switch to check that it was working, he led the way across the half-submerged remains of the causeway.

Tom and the children had disappeared by the time they reached the cave opening. From deep in the hillside the piping and the accompanying laughter continued. But not for long. There was a dull grating sound, followed by a thud – like a heavy door or rock sliding into place – and all at once the dark passage was deathly still.

'What was that?' Ross asked fearfully.

'I don't know.'

Ross stepped reluctantly into the tunnel, Angie close beside him. The pale light cast by the torch was hardly bright enough to guide their feet. Yet it was preferable to the otherwise engulfing darkness which lay ahead; and not without hesitation they ventured slowly forward.

Gradually, step by step, they left the comfort and the comparative security of the daylight behind them. The air within the tunnel smelled musty and stale; the walls on either side were slimy to the touch; while from above their heads there was a steady cold drip of moisture.

'We shouldn't go too far,' Ross murmured cautiously.

He had barely spoken when there was a suggestion of movement immediately ahead. He swung the torch upwards, and there, just discernible in the feeble circle of light, stood the figure of Tom.

'I see you have decided to join our little party after all,' he said with a frosty smile. He swept his hand ceremoniously to one side, as though inviting them to some splendid entertainment. 'Please come this way, my dears. You are more than welcome. There are some here, I might say, who are actually expecting you.'

But Ross and Angie were already backing away – Ross holding the torch out before him as though it were a weapon.

'What? Going already?' Tom went on mockingly. 'When the party has scarcely begun? Please reconsider, my pets. Some of us have been positively relishing the idea of your visit.'

Never had his voice sounded less inviting – somehow colder than the drops of water which fell from the low roof of the tunnel – and Ross and Angie turned and ran for the circle of daylight. They emerged from the tunnel together, slithered down the bank, and leaped across the causeway. Not until they had reached the safety of the trees did they look back. Crouched in the shelter of the fading bracken, they stared apprehensively

114

at the cave mouth. There was a brief delay, and then Tom appeared in the opening. He scanned the trees, failing to pick out their hiding place.

'What a pity,' he called in mournful tones. 'It would have been so much simpler had you come to us. Whereas this way we shall have to come to you. And we shall. Oh yes, don't doubt us. We shall.'

With a wave of the hand, he stepped back into the darkness.

TWO

'How long is it now?' Ross asked quietly.

They were crouched amidst withering ferns, effectively hidden from sight, but with a clear view of the opposite hillside.

'Over an hour,' Angie replied, glancing at her watch.

'Well it's about time . . .'

'Shhh!'

She laid a warning hand on his shoulder, drawing him further down into the ferns. On the far side of the river, Tom had again appeared at the mouth of the cave. His pipes were in his hand, as though in readiness, but he made no attempt to play them as he stepped into the open. It was soon clear why: despite the absence of music, the children continued to crowd at his heels, a steady stream of them issuing from the cave.

'Are they the same ones?' Ross whispered hopefully.

'What do you think?'

There was a bleak quality about Angie's reply which echoed his own sense of dread. The children who had entered the cave an hour earlier had been laughing and skipping excitedly. These were unnaturally silent, their faces as sombre and vacant as the cave mouth they had just left; and their movements, far from being joyful or excited, were deliberate, measured, totally devoid of emotion – more like the movements of puppets.

'What has he done with the others?' Ross murmured fearfully, half rising from the trampled nest of ferns.

His voice must have carried over the dull background noise of the river, for Tom looked up and stared directly at where he was crouching. He ducked down, convinced even as he flattened himself against the ferns that he had been seen. Yet Tom gave no sign of surprise or recognition, continuing to follow the path that led up into the trees.

'I could have sworn he spotted me,' Ross whispered.

He glanced at Angie, noticing for the first time that she was counting softly to herself.

'... twenty-three, twenty-four, twenty-five ...'

'What are you doing?'

She finished her count just as the last of the children disappeared into the woods.

'That's odd.'

'What is?'

'The number. One less than those who went in.'

'One less?' He thought he understood what was bothering her.

'But isn't that right? Remember we killed one of the rats. We took the piece of flesh with us.'

Angie shook her head.

'No, that isn't it. There should have been more. Don't you see? There's us and Nigel to be taken into account.'

She reached out and touched his neck at the point where the rat had bitten him.

He realized then what she was getting at – an idea he had been unconsciously blocking out for months now.

'But he hates us,' he objected.

'All the more reason for including us with the others.'

'Then why ...?'

But it wasn't a subject he could argue about dispassionately. He thrust his hand into his pocket, his fingers clasping the plastic barrel of the torch.

'Anyway,' he said belligerently, 'that's not what's important.

117

It's finding the others that matters.'

'Is it?' Angie asked in the same bleak tone she had used before. 'Do you really believe there's any point in looking?'

'But he couldn't just . . .!'

Ross lurched to his feet and blundered down through the tangle of brown fern. Angie, following as quickly as she could, caught up with him half way up the far slope.

'Think about Jack!' she said fiercely, tugging at his sleeve. 'What do you suppose Tom wanted him for? Isn't it because Jack is the original? An original he no longer needs?'

Ross turned to face her. 'But that was different!'

'How was it different?'

She clung to his arm, determined that he shouldn't enter the cave.

'There are so many this time!' he almost shouted.

'Which is why Tom daren't let them get away!'

'But Jack's old! These are so much younger!'

'Would that bother Tom? Would that mean anything to a creature.like him?'

He made as if to answer, then changed his mind. Jerking his arm free, he scrambled frantically up the slope.

'Ross!'

He had already disappeared into the mouth of the cave. Angie hurried after him, groping blindly in the gathering darkness. Her fingers closed on the loose cloth of his jacket and she pulled as hard as she could, trying vainly to yank him backwards.

'Do you really want to find out what he's done with them?' she pleaded. 'Can't you . . .?'

She never finished what she was trying to say. There was a faint click, as of rock striking against rock, and then the sound of her voice was obliterated by a tremendous explosion deep within the cave. The whole hillside seemed to shudder, threatening to slip down and crush them. And all at once Angie was no longer pulling at Ross's jacket: the two of them were clinging to each other in a fierce rush of wind, toppling over into the darkness together, while the rocky floor trembled crazily beneath them and the passage-way filled with noisy echoes and a choking cloud of dust.

'The torch!' Angie gasped out, coughing and fighting for breath.

'I've dropped it!' Ross swept a hand across the damp floor, his fingers striking the torch unexpectedly and sending it spinning off into the gloom. 'Oh no!'

He crawled after it, Angie close beside him, both of them groping frantically. It was Angie who found it.

'Here!' she panted, 'here!'

She fumbled awkwardly with the switch.

'Does it still work?'

'I'm not sure.' Her hands were shaking so much that she could barely control them. At her third attempt she managed to slide the plastic button forward. 'Yes . . . yes!'

The pale, wavering circle of light struggled feebly against the surrounding gloom. In those first few seconds all they could see was a drifting curtain of dust, an impenetrable gritty veil that swirled about them like a visible manifestation of the darkness. It cleared slowly, the torchlight probing through the swirling particles, penetrating further and further along the oval-shaped tunnel.

'Anybody there?' Ross called.

There was no answer. But through the settling dust, at the farthest extent of the torchlight, they saw something. A flicker of movement, a dimly discernible outline, which gradually resolved itself into three separate shapes.

'They're safe!' Ross burst out with relief.

'No, Ross! No!'

The light shifted and swung, playing erratically across the three advancing figures as Angie fought unsuccessfully to hold the torch steady. Step by step they drew closer, their bodies strangely pale and smooth.

'But they're . . . naked . . .!' Ross murmured uncertainly.

He snatched the torch from Angie's hands and crawled forward, trying to concentrate the dim beam on faces he already half recognized.

'Come back, Ross!' Angie wailed.

He could see them properly now: their dull lustreless eyes staring back at him, incuriously, like the cold unfeeling eyes of insects; their faces, all three of them, but one especially, as familiar to him as his own.

With a cry he dropped the torch, plunging the tunnel back into darkness. Something grabbed at his arm, and for a few blind moments of panic he tried to fight his way free – pushing and slapping hysterically at sinister tendrils which grappled with him.

'Ross, it's me!'

The mindless feeling of panic drained away, leaving him with Angie's warm fingers closed about his own. He gripped them tightly, the reassuring world of reason and sanity returning with a rush.

'Quick!' he managed to croak out.

Suddenly they were both running, stumbling hastily through the lingering curtain of dust – struggling for the second time that day to reach the safety of the open air.

Neither of them actually remembered emerging from the tunnel, nor crossing the river. They were far along the path, deep in the sheltering trees before the full reality of the autumn day, with its soft colours and cool moist breeze, finally broke in on them. They stopped running and stood quite still on the soft pathway. Yellowing leaves drifted down through the latticework of branches, landing noiselessly on the faded bracken.

'You saw them?' Ross said tentatively.

She nodded.

'The three that were missing?'

'Yes.'

Ross turned and looked searchingly back along the path. 'And the others?'

120

Angie said nothing, and it came to him with searing insight: a realization as sudden and irresistible as the explosion that had rocked the hillside; a bitter truth that temporarily eclipsed his vision of those three disturbingly familiar figures.

'The others!'

'Hush,' she whispered.

'They're gone, Angie!' He brushed one hand distractedly across his forehead, leaving a black smear on the startling pallor of his skin. 'We should have known, after what he said that night, down there beside the river. A mistake, he called it. His failure to get his hands on Jack – a mistake. Which he wouldn't make again. Not again.'

Angie, listening to him, shuddered slightly.

'But he was talking about us then,' she reminded him, 'you and me.'

A cool gust of wind rocked the branches above their heads, sending a flurry of leaves cascading down. In the stillness that followed, something moved stealthily amongst the trees: three pale shapes, silent and watchful, flitting rapidly from cover to cover.

THREE

He woke exactly as he had that night in summer, knowing instinctively he was not alone, that something near by was watching him – eyes furtively peering at him through the darkness. He sat up and switched on the bedside lamp. But this time there was nothing to be seen, the room bare and still, only the curtain stirring slightly at the half-open window.

'Who's there?' he whispered.

The breeze lifted the curtain, making it flap gently, while in the next room his father let out a loud snore and rolled over in his sleep. Everything seemed to be normal, nothing troubling the silence of the night, and Ross, after a last brief glance into the shadowy corners, lay back on the pillow. Only for a moment though: before he could close his eyes there was a warning knock on the wall. It was Angie's usual signal, yet tonight Ross detected something particularly urgent about it, and he swung himself out of bed and padded quickly across to the wall.

'Angie,' he murmured as loudly as he dared, his lips brushing the wallpaper, 'what's wrong?'

Her voice came through to him with surprising clarity, 'Ross! Quick!'

'Keep it down!'

'Outside, in the garden!'

He moved to the window and looked out. The sky was clear, the moon not far off the full. The lane, with its border of half-bare trees, was streaked with moonlight, a patchwork of black and silver which made it difficult to distinguish individual objects. He saw nothing unusual at first. Then, at the far edge of the lane, something stirred, and all at once two figures stood out from their background. They were as naked as they had been earlier in the day, their bodies paler than the moonlight, their faces lifted towards him, intent on the window at which he stood.

Angie's whisper reached him through the silence, 'Can you see them? They've been watching the cottage for at least ten minutes. I've been trying to wake you.'

Before he could answer, one of the figures – the one he feared most of all – crossed the lane and entered the garden. The weirdly familiar head and shoulders advanced deliberately up the path, passing directly below him, abruptly cut off from view by the overhanging kitchen roof. He waited and heard a faint rattle from downstairs as the kitchen door was tested. He had no fears for the door itself – it was old, but sturdy, and was always locked at night. Whereas the windows . . .!

He turned and scrambled across the room, half leaping, half falling down the narrow stairs. Even so, he was almost too late: the figure was there before him, peering incuriously into the dining room, one pale arm reaching through the gap, groping for the catch that held the window slightly ajar. Ross dashed around the table, knocked the catch free, and pulled the window to with a thud, trapping the arm between the frame and the sill. The pale fingers seemed to writhe in the half light, scrabbling ineffectually at the loose front of his pyjama jacket. They strained up towards his neck, their touch cool on his bare skin – and with an involuntary spasm of horror he shoved the window open. The ghostly reflection staggered away, the arm slithering back through the gap, and he slammed the window shut again, locking it securely.

He had not realized until then how near to panic he had been. His breathing was unnaturally loud in the silence of the room, his body drenched with sweat. He wiped his sleeve across his forehead and looked directly at this perfect replica of himself. The eyes stared back at him through the thin pane of glass, cool, incurious, appraising. They showed none of the fear, none of the panic, which he felt so strongly. For all their likeness to his own, they were alien eyes, the eyes of a total stranger. Gazing at them, Ross suddenly felt much steadier. It occurred to him that this figure was not really his double at all: behind the superficial similarities there lurked a being wholly different from himself. A vast gulf of understanding and feeling separated them. And with that realization came a sense of calm, much of his dread and uncertainty draining from him. This person or thing now facing him was in itself no more daunting or threatening than Tom; it was merely another aspect of the same unknown force that had brought Tom into being – a force which, in some inexplicable way, emanated from the hollow in the woods.

'You're not driving me out the way you did Jack,' Ross murmured deliberately.

It was, as far as he was concerned, a statement of fact, not just an expression of bravado. And for a moment it appeared that the naked figure outside accepted the statement. With a slight inclination of the head, as of defeat, it backed away – two ... three paces. But instead of leaving the garden, it glanced upwards. The edge of the steeply sloping roof was just out of reach, and with an abrupt movement it sprang for the gutter.

This time Ross was better prepared for such a move. Without panic, he ran up the stairs. Again he barely reached the open window in time. Both pale hands were already gripping the ledge, while from the other side of the intervening wall Angie's urgent whispers sounded a warning. A few seconds more and the head and shoulders would have forced their way into the room. Before that could happen, Ross grabbed for the top of the window intending to slam it down; but at the very last moment

124

he relented, unwilling even then to damage fingers so uncannily like his own. Instead, he stamped lightly on each of the clutching hands with the bare heel of his foot. It was all that was needed: the fingers jerked open and the slope of the roof did the rest. There was a faint cry and a frantic slithering sound – the final thump of the body hitting the ground drowned out by the crash of the hastily closed window.

Ross thankfully slipped the catch into the locked position and leaned his damp forehead against the cool glass. But not for long. The darkness of the room was suddenly shattered by a blaze of light; and Ross, totally confused, whirled around to find a tall figure standing in the open doorway.

'No! Keep back!' he yelled.

Bill Miller, his hair tousled, his face puffy with sleep, strode across the room and cuffed him on the side of the head. 'What on earth are you up to, boy?' he shouted.

Caught off guard, Ross could only stare blankly at his father's face. 'What's that, Dad?' he asked stupidly.

'I want to know what you're up to!' Bill Miller repeated, an edge of anger to his voice.

Without stopping to think, Ross pointed through the window at the shadowy garden. 'Down there!' he said excitedly. 'They're down there! Exactly like Angie and me!'

'Are you having me on, boy?'

Months earlier, he and Angie had decided that there was no point in trying to explain things to their parents. But now, badly shaken by the events of the past few minutes, he found himself blurting it all out. 'It's Tom, he made them, in the caves by the river. Two of them that look like Angie and me.'

'Tom?'

'Yes, the one like Jack. Except he isn't. He's a clone too. Something wants him and us ... not the real people ... just copies. That's why Jack chopped off his finger ... and why the rats came ... to collect samples of skin. So Tom could play his flute later. Like the pied piper ... but not the real pied piper either. A meat dealer is what Jack calls him. Because ...'

Bill Miller again slapped his son on the side of the head. 'Have you gone barmy or something?'

Ross blinked rapidly and shook his head. 'Sorry, Dad. I ... I must have been having a dream.'

'More like a nightmare by the sound of it.'

'Yes ... I suppose so ... a nightmare.'

'Well snap out of it! I've never heard so much nonsense in all my life. If you ask me, it's all that reading they get you to do at school. Filling your head with a lot of daft ideas.'

Ross rubbed the side of his head. 'I'm awake now, Dad.'

'You'd better be, my boy! I don't want to be disturbed again.'

He stomped over to the door and clicked off the light. But just as he was about to cross the landing he glanced back into the darkened room. 'You sure you're all right now?' he said in a more kindly voice.

In spite of himself, Ross again felt the urge to confess everything, to shift the burden of responsibility to his father. He had a momentary vision of the whole affair being taken out of his hands – of the police being called in, of Tom being arrested, of ... The obvious absurdity of such hopes crowded in on him.

'I'm fine, Dad.'

He heard his father climb back into bed and settle himself for sleep. When the house was again silent he went to the window and peered out. As far as he could make out, the garden was deserted, as was the lane and field. But what of the woods beyond, showing now as a dark smudge in the moonlight? And that place beyond the woods, the rising ground above the cave, more like a burial mound than a simple hillside?

Ross brushed his lips lightly against the cool glass pane. 'A nightmare,' he murmured softly.

FOUR

They were standing in a group just inside the school gates, more than twenty of them, distinguishable from the other children only by their pale faces, unweathered as yet by sun or wind.

'They're waiting for us,' Nigel said in a horrified whisper, 'the way that . . . that other one was last night!'

He turned away from the corridor window, his eyes round with fright, his thin lips trembling.

'You should have seen him, Ross,' he went on in an agitated voice, 'he was watching all night. I didn't get a wink of sleep, and Mum wouldn't believe me. Whenever I called her he hid. But he was there, every time I looked. He . . .'

'All right, Shrimp,' Ross broke in, 'we've been over all that before. It wasn't any different for us, you know.'

'But he was waiting for me. And now those other ones, out there, they're . . . they're . . .'

His eyes, behind the glasses, seemed to blur and dim, and Angie, silent until then, walked over and put her arm around his shoulder.

'Crying won't help matters, Nigel,' she said gently, 'nor arguing amongst ourselves. What we have to do is find a safe way of getting out of here.'

'Such as how?' Ross asked.

She pursed her lips.

'An escort would help.'

'A what?'

'Someone to get us safely through the gates. Here, this one'll do.'

One of the male teachers came walking along the corridor, briefcase in hand. As he pushed open the main door, Angie stepped up beside him, Ross and Nigel close behind.

'Could I have a word with you, Mr Webb?' she asked politely.

He glanced at her through heavy-rimmed spectacles. 'I'm in a bit of a hurry right now, Angie.'

'Oh, I won't hold you up.'

The four of them emerged into the playground and the waiting crowd, after an initial hesitation, moved forward to block the exit into the street.

'Well?' – Mr Webb, oblivious of the menace in the pale, watchful faces, made his way briskly towards the gates.

'It's about . . . about tonight's homework,' Angie stammered out, improvising wildly.

'Well, what about it?'

'I wondered if you could let me off this once.'

The crowd gave way reluctantly, drawing aside just enough to let the teacher through.

'What's this, a guard of honour?' Mr Webb asked jovially. And then to Angie, 'I suppose you have a reason for this request.'

'Oh yes.'

She squeezed past him, ignoring the baleful stares which followed her. There was a sharp cry from behind as Ross jerked the terrified Nigel clear of pale clutching hands.

'What's going on back there?' Mr Webb turned to face the crowd.

'Er . . . excuse me, Sir.'

Ross, half dragging Nigel, pushed the teacher roughly aside and staggered out into the street after Angie.

'Look here, what do you think you're up to?' Mr Webb protested, an expression of bewilderment on his face.

The whole crowd was now milling about him.

'If this is supposed to be some kind of joke!'

Ross drew the gate closed with a clang, and the teacher, retreating before the half circle of intent faces, backed into the heavy iron bars. It was exactly the opportunity the three fugitives needed. Darting across the busy highway, they turned down the nearest side road and ran for all they were worth. Not until they were well clear of the school did they slow down.

'What now?' Angie asked.

Nigel, having regained his breath, began to cry again. 'I want to go home,' he wailed. 'My mum'll look after me.'

'I wouldn't be too sure of that, Shrimp.'

They had come as far as Elm Walk. The tall trees, with most of their leaves already fallen, presented an odd picture of life and death; their once withered outer limbs, stricken by disease, now covered with a bristle of fresh young branches. The three children stood facing each other in the cross-hatched shadow cast by the trees.

'You can't stop me going home,' Nigel whimpered.

'No one's stopping you,' Angie said. 'Ross is just warning you that it may not be safe there either.'

'But my mum . . .'

'That figure you saw last night,' Ross interrupted him, 'where d'you think it is now?'

There was a sudden hush.

'You don't think it . . . it . . .?'

'That's what we have to find out.'

They said nothing more, continuing towards their homes, pausing only when they reached the end of the lane.

'There's no need for us all to take a risk,' Ross said, 'one's enough.'

'In that case,' Angie said firmly, 'it'd better be me.'

Ross stepped in front of her. 'You seem to have forgotten something,' he said with forced lightness. 'You're the brains around here. We have to look after you, because brains are what we need to get out of this.'

'I suppose that means I'm not capable,' she answered caustically.

He grinned at her. 'No, it's just that I can run faster.'

She shrugged, reluctantly conceding the point, and he stole off down the lane. As he entered his own back garden Mrs Bowles emerged from the neighbouring cottage.

'Ah Ross,' she said pleasantly, 'you're looking a lot better I'm glad to say.'

'What?'

He was so surprised by her changed attitude that he stopped in the middle of the path.

'I said you're looking much better.'

'Me?' he asked, bewildered. 'What are you getting at?'

She drew back, affronted by his tone. 'Well, I see you didn't take long to revert to type,' she said haughtily. 'I was beginning to hope, after our little chat this morning, that you have some manners after all. But I see I was mistaken.'

'Our little chat?'

He looked past Mrs Bowles to where another figure had appeared on the back step – so like the Angie he knew and yet so different, the eyes frosty cold. That incurious stare told him all he needed to know, and with a single bound he reached the back door and burst into the house.

The kitchen and the living room were deserted, but as he placed his foot on the bottom stair there was a faint sound overhead and a figure stepped out onto the narrow landing above.

'Don't move,' his own voice murmured to him softly.

Involuntarily he froze. It was, he realized dimly, what he was intended to do – to stand there mesmerized, rendered helpless by the sheer uncanny quality of the situation. The stairwell no longer simply a part of the house: transformed temporarily into a reflecting mirror, reproducing not only his face, his clothes,

130

his gestures, but even the sound of his voice. The figure, confident of its own power, descended slowly, the mirror magically taking on a life of its own. Himself still, yet with one difference. Something glinted in the right hand, something thin and sharply pointed – and with a start of deeper recognition Ross broke free.

'What are you?' he said loudly. 'The messenger boy?'

The figure faltered briefly.

'Well in that case,' Ross added hurriedly, 'you'd better take a message. Tell him – whatever sent you – that Jack's alive and well. And so are we.'

The hand holding the knife jerked upwards, but Ross was already scrambling back through the kitchen and out into the garden.

Angie and Nigel were waiting for him outside the gate, and in his haste he almost made a mistake.

'What are you doing . . .?' he began.

Her hand snaked out, clutching for his hair, and he dodged aside just in time. Ducking under her arm, he shoved her away so that she cannoned into Nigel, the two of them sprawling full length in the lane. She half rose and crouched facing him as he edged around her. Her eyes, he noticed with a shudder, registered no emotion, no anger or hatred, staring at him much as he might have stared at an insignificant plant.

'There's no point in running,' she said, her voice oddly neutral, 'because you can't stop it now.'

He hesitated in spite of himself, although he recognized that this too was a delaying tactic.

'What can't I stop?'

'The growing. It will go on now, no matter what you do.'

'What kind of growing?'

'*The* growing.'

Her body, tense and still, suddenly lunged at him, her outstretched hand grasping him about the ankle. He tried to tear himself free, but she held on with bewildering strength, her fingers biting into his flesh like talons – the accumulated energy of her young body somehow concentrated into that one purposeful grasp. He looked wildly about him and saw with a sinking heart that all the cottage gardens were empty.

'Still him!' she said softly.

Nigel had already risen to his feet, and, with a frantic savagery that alarmed even himself, Ross brought his other foot violently down onto her wrist, breaking her hold and grinding her hand brutally into the hard gravelly surface of the lane. Then he was running desperately, back to where the real Angie and Nigel were waiting for him near Jack's cottage.

'They were there!' he gasped out.

'I know,' Angie said in a frightened voice, 'we saw it happen.'

'So what are we standing here for?'

He turned in the direction of Angie's pointing finger. A group of children had just entered the near end of the lane.

'I want to go home!' Nigel sobbed.

Ross, moved by a sudden irrational anger, grabbed him by the shoulders and shook him like a rag doll. 'You haven't got any home!' he yelled. 'Can't you get that into your head? You're redundant! You're just the spare they want to get rid of!'

Angie forced the two of them apart. 'For goodness sake, Ross! Use your head. Let's get out of here. We can lose them in the woods.'

The advancing group had broken into a run.

'That's their place!' he objected frantically, 'where they belong!'

'And I suppose this isn't!'

She was already clambering over the fence, and Ross, after a last desperate glance over his shoulder, grabbed Nigel by the scruff of the neck and the seat of his trousers.

'But Mum'll be expecting me!' he protested. 'She'll know the difference! She ...'

Ross heaved with all his strength, half throwing, half

132

tumbling Nigel over the wooden palings. Seconds later the three of them were running for the sanctuary of the trees.

FIVE

They emerged from the woods near the edge of the valley and ran silently across a short stretch of open pasture towards the highway. It had begun to rain lightly, a fine mist that drifted down onto their bare heads, beading their hair and clothes with glistening droplets.

'We seem to have lost them,' Angie said, having to raise her voice above the roar of the passing traffic.

'Looks like it.'

'But we're getting wet out here,' Nigel complained.

'That's the least of our worries, Shrimp.'

Taking Nigel by the arm, he urged him across the highway, the three of them darting hazardously between the speeding cars.

'You trying to kill me or something?' Nigel almost screamed.

'I'm trying to keep you alive, though don't ask me why.'

He pushed the younger boy away disdainfully and followed Angie up the steep chalky bank that marked the beginning of the downs.

'Come on, Nigel,' Angie said more kindly, 'not far now. We're taking you somewhere safe, where Jack's been all along.'

At the mention of Jack's name, Nigel, scrambling up the last part of the bank, stopped in his tracks. 'Not him! You saw what

134

he did that day, to my glasses.'

Ross reached down and jerked Nigel up beside him. 'That wasn't Jack, you idiot! Any more than those three figures back there are really us. The real Jack got away months ago.'

Nigel stared at them both blankly. 'I ... I don't ... understand,' he said with trembling lips.

Angie wiped the wet hair away from his forehead. 'Don't worry,' she said encouragingly. 'You just stay close to me and I'll explain what I can.'

They trudged on over the even curve of the downs, Angie talking slowly and patiently, the rain growing steadily harder. By the time they reached the quarry, half an hour later, the earlier fine mist had developed into a heavy downpour, plastering their hair and clothes to their shivering bodies. The quarry itself, seen through a curtain of rain, was a dismal sight, its bare chalk walls stained a grey putty colour, many of its narrow valleys half flooded, isolated tussocks of grass barely showing above the black sheen of water.

'I've heard about this place,' Nigel broke out. 'My mum says it's a death trap. She reckons some of those chalk cliffs could cave in and bury you.'

'So what?' Ross answered indifferently. 'Right now it's a darned sight less dangerous than that village back there.'

'But what if one of those cliffs collapses on us?'

'Then we won't have much to worry about, will we?'

He and Angie picked their way down towards the gates, and Nigel, after an initial hesitation, scrambled after them. He continued to grumble about the dangers of the quarry, but they ignored him, climbing wearily over the gates and splashing through the puddles towards the hut.

Jack was sitting just inside the door, draped in his heavy overcoat. His face lit up at the sight of them.

'What's this then?' he crowed delightedly. 'And young Shrimp as well! Must be my birthday. Three visitors no less, and on a day like this. Three to visit their old mate through all this pitter-patter raindrops falling.'

'We're not visitors, Jack,' Ross corrected him. 'We're here to stay, like you.'

A look of bewilderment flitted across Jack's face. He stood up, trying to peer past them. 'Where's the others, then? They lagging behind?'

'There aren't any others, Jack. Just us three.'

'But all them others that the rats nipped. Boys and girls all. Regular players they would have been, full of fun and games. They must be somewhere!'

'They're gone, Jack.'

'Gone, d'you say? You mean he ... he got them?'

Ross and Angie nodded dumbly.

'Gone? But they ... they ...'

Jack stumbled out into the rain and squatted forlornly at the front of the hut, his head leant back against the grey weatherboard.

'Boys and girls come out to play,' he croaked. *'Boys and girls come out ... come out ...'*

The rain was streaming down his sunken stubbly cheeks, making it impossible to say whether he was crying. But his eyes were red-rimmed and oddly filmed over.

'You shouldn't sit out here,' Ross said gently, crouching beside him.

Jack blinked hard several times.

'No!' he said with sudden vehemence. 'I don't belong out here, that's a fact! It's not the place for yours truly. Hideaway Jack, that's me. Tucked up in his hole like a mouse, no more trouble than a wee trembling mouse.'

'What happened isn't your fault, Jack.'

'Says you!'

He stood up abruptly, throwing off Ross's restraining hand, and shuffled back into the hut. Ignoring Angie and Nigel, he headed straight for the low bed in the corner and lay down.

'Hideaway Jack,' he mumbled disconsolately, 'old hideaway.'

His eyes were tightly closed now, his knees pulled up almost to his chin.

'Hush,' Ross murmured.

He stood helplessly beside the bed, gazing down at the huddled form. Within minutes the old man was asleep, though still with a troubled expression on his face.

Ross turned to Angie and Nigel. 'It's been a terrible shock for him,' he said apologetically. 'He'll get things straight when he's had a sleep.'

Angie was standing shivering in the corner, both hands clasped about her shoulders. 'Maybe he's got things straight already,' she said thoughtfully. 'After all, he is hiding away.'

'But that isn't the point, Angie. He's blaming himself for what's happened. He thinks he's useless.'

Angie gave a barely perceptible shake of the head. 'No, it's you who's missing the point, Ross. He is useless, and so are we. What can we do here? Except wait. And for what?'

'But we had to get away. We needed time.'

'That's what I've been trying to tell myself. But I keep coming back to the same question. Time for what?'

'To think. To decide how best to ... to ...' – he stumbled to a halt.

'What's going on?' Nigel asked in a worried voice.

Angie went to the door and gazed out, too preoccupied to answer him.

'Time,' she said reflectively. 'Three or four days at the most before our food runs out. Perhaps even less if ...'

She stopped, her whole body suddenly stiffening.

'What's the matter?' Ross asked.

She drew back into the shadowy portion of the hut. 'Up there, on the cliff!'

Ross and Nigel followed her gaze. At the far side of the valley, high above them, was Ross's double. Even in the fading light and driving rain, the outline was unmistakable. He was standing

137

at the edge of the chalk cliff, staring down at them.

'You promised we'd be safe here!' Nigel cried. 'You promised!'

Ross clamped a hand over Nigel's mouth, silencing him.

'We'll have to do something now,' Angie said in a strained whisper.

SIX

The single candle cast a warm yellow glow over the walls of the hut. The door was closed, a square of hessian nailed across the window. In the corner Jack slept on, his mouth open, his face slightly furrowed with concern.

'Is he still out there?' Angie whispered.

Ross crept to the door and peered through a crack between two planks. The rain had stopped and the moon, only one day off the full, bathed the chalk valley in a bluish-white light. Clearly visible against the skyline was his own hunched shape.

'He hasn't moved,' he answered, squatting beside Angie on the dusty wooden floor. 'What puzzles me is why he just waits around. You'd think, now he's found us, he'd go off and get some help.'

'Perhaps he doesn't need to,' Angie said. 'He may be able to communicate over a distance. Despite the way he looks, he has more in common with whatever it was that made the music months ago. And that thing had no trouble projecting its commands for quite a long way.'

'So you think he's already sent out some kind of signal?'

'Don't you? Anyway, we'll know by morning. Which gives us only a matter of hours to work out what's happening.'

'You mean we're just going to sit here and talk?' Nigel said incredulously. They were the first words he had uttered for some time. Ever since darkness had fallen, he had been crouched at the far end of the hut looking cold and frightened.

'What do you expect us to do?' Ross asked. 'Go out and tackle him? I've already had one run-in with them, back there in the lane, and I don't want a repeat performance. They're a lot stronger than we are.'

'How can they be? If they're really a copy, they should be the same in every way.'

'Not necessarily,' Angie explained. 'Strength isn't just a matter of muscle. It starts in your head. It has a lot to do with the way you direct your energy. And at that level we're no match for them.'

'We haven't got a chance then,' Nigel said miserably. 'That's what you're saying, isn't it?' He choked back a sob and wiped his nose on his still sodden sleeve.

'I'm not suggesting we should give in,' Angie corrected him.'But I do think we have to decide on the best way of opposing them. And we can't really do that until we work out what their purpose is.'

'Fat lot of chance we have of doing that,' Nigel whimpered.

Angie turned to Ross. 'Any ideas?'

There was a brief silence during which a tiny moth, spiralling jerkily about the candle, ventured too close to the flame and went careering off into the darkness, its wings casting grotesque shadows over the walls.

'I don't know if this is going to help,' Ross said hesitantly, 'but one thing's been puzzling me for quite a while. We know there's something in the woods that's alien to us – that much at least I can understand. What I don't understand is the way it's acting. For instance, if that thing is so different from human beings, why is it so preoccupied with us? Why try and copy our ways and appearance?'

'Because we're the dominant species, Ross. It can hardly ignore us, pretend we aren't here.'

Ross shook his head in frustration. 'No, that isn't what I'm trying to say. Think back to the day we went to the hollow and met Tom. He made it pretty plain then that he detested all animal life, everything made of flesh and blood. It was the vegetation, the trees especially, that he liked. Yet the next thing he did was help create human-type creatures. More flesh and blood. The very beings he's up against. Isn't that a sort of contradiction?'

Angie gazed dubiously at the far wall. 'Perhaps he, or whatever's doing the thinking, believes that you have to fight fire with fire; that pitting human beings against themselves is the best way of destroying the species.'

'But it isn't!' Ross exclaimed. 'If that thing in the woods had just wanted to destroy human beings, it could have done it without having to clone them. All Tom had to do was blow on his pipes and those kids would've followed him without question. It was the same with us when we first heard the music: we had no will of our own. The music alone could have lured the whole village over the edge of a cliff. But it didn't.'

Angie nodded. 'Yes, something took great pains to keep the number of people in the village constant, so no one would notice anything was going on. That's why Tom wanted to find Jack – to eliminate him – and why we're being hunted down. We're duplicates. We could give the game away.'

'But what game?' Ross objected. 'Does it make sense? Why not just finish us off and be done with it?'

Angie reached out and picked up a piece of newly fallen wax, compressing it first into a ball, then flattening it between forefinger and thumb. 'In some special kind of way,' she said slowly, 'we must be needed. Our bodies anyway.'

'Needed?'

'Yes. What does Jack call that thing in the woods? The meat man. That makes good sense. To him we're parcels of meat. But not that only. We're also creatures he has a use for. He must have. Why else would he create duplicates?'

'But why us? Why not use animals? Or better still, trees and bushes? He doesn't object to them. Look at the way the countryside blossomed this year. That must have been his doing.'

Angie took another piece of wax from the candle, broke it into fragments and added legs and arms to the existing disc. She held the finished article up for Ross to see – a crude headless replica of a human being.

'There must be something special about humans,' she said speculatively, 'even from his point of view. What do you suppose it is? Something that distinguishes us from every other life form?'

'Normally I'd reckon it was our brains,' he said, 'but not in this case. Our brain is the one part of us that hasn't been copied.'

'What could it be then?' Angie said softly, putting the question as much to herself as to Ross. 'What else makes us unique?'

They both fell silent, and for a while the only sound in the hut was Jack's regular breathing. To the surprise of both of them, it was Nigel who broke the silence.

'If you ask me the answer's obvious.'

'Here we go,' Ross groaned, 'boy-wonder on the job.'

Nigel shuffled forward, his spectacles catching and reflecting the light of the candle. 'But it is obvious,' he insisted. 'They're always going on about it on those nature programmes on the telly. We're the only species inhabiting every part of the planet.'

'And that's your big solution? I might have guessed . . .'

'No, hold on,' Angie broke in. 'I think he could be right. We're the most adaptable creatures on earth. And also the most mobile. That's probably what makes us useful. Our ability to go everywhere and anywhere.'

'What's so useful about that?'

'Well for a start it would make us perfect messengers. Yes!

142

Messengers or ... carriers of some kind!'

'Carriers of what?'

Some of the eagerness and excitement faded from Angie's eyes. 'That's what we still have to discover,' she said more soberly.

Nigel, his face splotched with tear stains, sniggered unpleasantly and edged back into the shadows. 'I told you so,' he said. 'It's a lot of useless talk. All your suppose-this and suppose-that, and where does it get us? He's up there on the cliff the same as before and we're stuck in here. We're right back where we started from.'

'D'you think so?' Angie answered coolly.

She stood up and went to the door, apparently assuring herself that Ross's double was still there.

'At least I'm reasonably confident about one thing,' she said, turning back towards the light. 'That figure out there is carrying something. Whether it's in his head, his body, or his clothing, we don't know. But if we can make him give up that one secret, we have a chance.'

SEVEN

Ross woke with a start as a thin pencil of light touched his face. He sat up, feeling stiff and groggy, and rubbed his eyes. It seemed only moments ago that Nigel had been complaining he would never get to sleep. Yet already it was morning, with narrow shafts of sunlight streaming through the tears and holes in the hessian that covered the side window.

Taking care not to disturb the others, he crept noiselessly to the door (still crudely barricaded with a chair and planks of wood) and put his eye to the crack. As he had feared, the figure on the cliff was no longer alone: he had been joined by a girl and by a younger boy, shorter and with spectacles that glinted in the sunlight.

There was a movement behind him and Angie asked quietly, 'How many?'

'Three out of four. Only Tom is missing.'

'You think he'll come too?'

'I expect so. There'll be one for each of us then.'

He had tried to keep his voice low, but Nigel moved restlessly in the corner.

'What's happening?' He sat up, one side of his face grey with dust from the floor.

'Nothing yet. But there are three of them out there now.'

'Is one of them . . . me?'

144

'I'm afraid so, Shrimp.'

He was prepared for Nigel to start whining and complaining, as he had on the previous day, but instead a sly look came into the younger boy's eyes.

'I was thinking about this last night,' he said, 'when you two were nattering on. And I decided then, he's never going to catch me. D'you know why? Because if he's a copy, he'll have bad eyes too. And I'm the one with the glasses. Without these he won't be able to see much.'

He grinned owlishly at them.

'I'm sorry, Shrimp,' Ross answered, 'but it won't work out that way.'

'Why not? Those other two are your problem, not mine. What d'you expect me to do, stick around and help you out? When I've got a chance of escaping?'

'You haven't got any more of a chance than we have. That figure out there, he's wearing glasses like yours.'

'But he can't be!' Nigel scrambled over to the door. 'Damn him! Damn his rotten eyes! He's got my busted pair, that Mum fixed with tape!'

'Not so loud,' Angie advised him.

But her warning came too late. Jack, startled from more than twelve hours of shocked, deeply withdrawn sleep, suddenly sat up and swung himself off the bed. Still half drugged, he staggered across the hut and nearly fell.

'Where . . .?' he said in a bewildered voice, his eyes swinging crazily to and fro, 'Where . . .?'

Ross took his arm, steadying him. 'It's all right, Jack. You've had a sleep, that's all.'

Jack's vision cleared enough for him to see a small boy crouching beside the door, and he reached out one quivering hand.

'They're here, are they, Ross lad?'

'Who, Jack?'

'Them, the others.'

'He means the kids,' Angie said quietly.

'No, Jack, I told you, they're gone.'

'Gone?'

He lunged wildly at the door and with a single sweep of his arm tore away the flimsy barricade. The door, no longer pinned shut, swung open on its single hinge, flooding the interior of the hut with morning light. Hazily, through the brilliant glare, Jack saw the three figures on the cliff top, and with an inarticulate cry he sprang through the opening and ran across the valley floor, his ragged coat-tails streaming out behind him.

'Boys and girls,' he shouted joyously, *'boys and girls come out to . . .'*

But long before he could reach the base of the cliff he was met by a barrage of heavy stones. The first struck him a glancing blow on the temple and he went down, head cradled in his arms, while other stones thudded on the ground around him.

'Jack!' Ross shouted.

He sprinted across the valley, dodging as best he could the stones now aimed in his direction. One hit him a sickening blow on the chest and he nearly fell; but he recovered quickly, heaving Jack to his feet and dragging him back towards the hut.

'Quick!' he gasped out, 'those old bandages we left here! Anything!'

Blood was streaming down the side of Jack's face, and Angie, after scrabbling in the box beside the bed, clamped a handful of clean rags over the wound.

'Take it easy, Jack,' she said gently, helping Ross lower him onto the bed.

The old man brushed a hand across his balding head and gave each of them a level look, his eyes suddenly steady, his face composed.

'It wasn't them, was it, Ross boy?'

'No, Jack.'

'It was the green piper's doing, isn't that right? The rats' leavings? Them that the meat man sent?'

Ross nodded and glanced at Nigel.

'Don't just stand there, Shrimp!' he barked out. 'Get the door closed!'

'Not me!'

He swung around. Nigel was standing against the side wall, his whole body rigid with fright, flecks of foam at the corners of his mouth.

'I said shut it!'

'Not me!' Nigel babbled. 'I'm not the one they're after. It's him! Jack! He's the one they want.'

'Don't be a fool!'

'Well they can have him as far as I'm concerned. Don't ask me to stay in this death trap!'

Before Ross could stop him, he darted through the doorway and ran from the hut. Again a shower of stones rained down from the cliff top, falling just short of him. He stopped, totally confused, blinking nervously in the sunlight. Then, having apparently lost all sense of direction, he turned to the left and ran off into the maze of valleys that criss-crossed the enclosed area of the quarry.

'He won't have a chance in there on his own!' Angie burst out. 'We'll have to help him!'

'What about Jack?'

The old man pushed them gently away. 'I'm fine now,' he said in a steady voice.

'But what if they come while we're away?'

'I'll be ready for them this time,' Jack said, and he reached over to the window-sill and picked up the axe. 'Just let them try anything,' he added meaningfully.

Ross wavered and gave in. 'All right. But barricade the door behind us.'

He and Angie ran outside, keeping well clear of the cliff. Only two figures stood up there now, the smallest of the three having disappeared.

'He must be after Nigel,' Angie said. 'Let's hope we can reach him first.'

Side by side, they ran along the twisting, narrowing valley, splashing through the murky puddles, pausing briefly at every intersection to shout Nigel's name. Soon they were deep into the quarry, surrounded by a putty-grey world of damp chalk. It was a forbidding enough place on such a morning, with everything still sodden from the previous day's rain, many of the narrow valleys almost blocked by cave-ins and slips. Some of the slips were obviously fresh, parts of the cliff, saturated with rain, having collapsed during the night. It was on one of these recent mounds of chalky rubble that they first saw Nigel's footprints.

'This way,' Ross panted.

They clambered over the obstruction and found themselves in a deep, steep-sided cleft. They ran on, rounding the nearest bend just in time to see Nigel disappear from view a short distance ahead. Never very athletic or strong, he was already tirèd, his initial frantic flight now reduced to a plodding run.

They increased their pace and soon caught sight of him again. But now he was not alone. Above him, skirting the edge of the defile and matching him stride for stride, was his double.

'Wait!' Angie shouted.

Nigel glanced back and saw, not Angie and Ross, but the figure now shadowing his every move. He gave a short piercing scream and turned wildly to his right, scrambling over a heap of crumbling chalk and slithering down into an even narrower defile. Too late, he realized he had blundered into a cul-de-sac. There was no going back: the figure had stopped and was crouched at the very edge of the cutting, ready to slide down and block his retreat. Ahead of him lay an almost vertical wall of chalk. Only at one point, slightly to his right, was there a possible escape route: a series of eroded ledges, like the steps of an ancient, gigantic staircase, leading up to the open downland.

Oblivious of Ross's urgent cries, he ran straight for this point. His forward impetus carried him up and over the first few ledges; thereafter he had to struggle the rest of the way, grabbing at outcrops of flint or chalk that broke off in his hands, constantly fighting for precarious footholds. Somehow, miraculously, he reached the top. But as he grasped the overhanging lip of grass and pulled himself up, there was a thud of footsteps and his own familiar face confronted him.

'Nigel! Look out!' Ross and Angie yelled in unison.

Powerless to intervene, they watched as the two identical figures met in a fierce embrace. Locked together, they staggered towards the cliff's edge, their feet slipping on the wet grass. One of them was screaming in terror, but it was no longer clear which.

'I can't tell them apart!' Angie said in an agonized voice.

The nearer of the figures broke free and stepped backwards. He stood poised for a split second at the very brink of the grassy overhang. Then the chalk cliff beneath, soaked by the long hours of rain, bulged outwards and shifted, cascading down into the valley with a faint roar. Nigel's blank, pinched face swung round towards them, his two hands clutching feebly at the air, and in a twisting dive he plunged forward into space. He fell a considerable distance before landing head-first on the hard chalky slope: so that when he finally rolled and tumbled his way to the valley floor, he looked more like an untidy bundle of clothes than a human being.

Angie bent over the broken body. 'Which is it?' she whispered fearfully.

Ross looked from the body to the figure above and back again. Near to where Angie was crouching something glinted amidst the rubble. He went over and picked up a pair of shattered glasses. They were bent and twisted, but still held together across the bridge by a tape binding.

'We'd better get you down from there, Nigel,' he called out, relief evident in his voice.

In thankful silence he clambered up over the ledges and helped the younger boy make the difficult descent. At the

149

bottom, all three of them stood around the limp, contorted body
– Nigel still with shaking hands and a face grey-white with
shock.

'Is he ... is he ...?' he asked uncertainly.

'Yes, he's dead,' Angie said softly.

The apparently lifeless face, as though responding to their
voices, suddenly twitched.

'Hey! Wait a minute!' Ross broke out.

It twitched again, and very slowly, tentatively, something
emerged from one of the nostrils.

'What the hell!'

They moved backwards, instinctively, as a thin green tendril
slithered clear of the nostril. The mouth jerked open abruptly,
and another, slightly thicker tendril pushed its way out over the
lips. Two more green shoots emerged from the ears. They grew
visibly, distorting the features of the face as they lengthened and
thickened, snaking and coiling like fingers of bindweed as they
sought for some purchase. One by one, the sensitive greenish-
white tips reached the ground and prodded delicately amongst
the rubble.

'What's it looking for?' Angie asked in a horrified whisper.

The tendrils continued to prod and search, but when they
encountered nothing but chalk and flint, they seemed to give
up, drawing back, settling in coils across the bloated face like
eyeless green snakes.

'I don't know about you two,' Ross said grimly, 'but I'm going
to put a stop to this.'

He had taken a penknife from his pocket. But before he could
open it, two figures, his own and Angie's doubles, entered the
valley behind them.

'Watch out!' Angie murmured.

She backed away, both arms wrapped protectively around
Nigel. Pushed beyond endurance, he could do no more than
cling to her, whimpering pitifully, his face buried in her
shoulder. Ross picked up a jagged piece of flint before he also

150

backed off.

'Two can play at your little game,' he said threateningly.

But the advancing figures barely looked at them. They had eyes, it seemed, only for their dead companion. With a care which bordered on tenderness, their faces as pale and expressionless as ever, they lifted the body between them and carried it from the valley.

EIGHT

Ross slithered down the slope towards the hut where the others were waiting.

'They've gone all right,' he said. 'Heading in the direction of the village.'

'More's the pity, I say,' Jack mumbled menacingly.

He spat on the axe head, continuing to hone the edge with a smooth piece of flint.

'D'you reckon they'll come back?' Nigel asked.

His face, despite the grime and dust, was unnaturally pale, with dark purplish smudges beneath the eyes.

'Who knows?' Ross said.

'Well can't we leave now? Please, Ross, just in case.'

'After what we saw back there, I'm not too keen on sticking around either, Shrimp.' He looked quizzically at Jack. 'D'you know any other good hiding places? Preferably well away from here.'

Jack shook his head stubbornly. 'No more hide and seek,' he muttered. 'No more blind man's buff. No more piggy in the middle.' He again spat on the discoloured metal. 'And do you know why?'

'Why, Jack?'

'For a lot of good reasons, boys and girls both.' He held up his hand, showing the scarred stump where the finger had been.

'And my old pointer, there's another reason for you.'

'But what about us?' Ross argued. 'Shouldn't we look after ourselves?'

'They'll get us anyway, Ross lad. Unless we find him – the meat man, the rat caller, the old green piper himself.'

Ross turned to Angie for support. 'What do you think?'

'Jack's right. They're certain to catch up with us.'

'Even if we hid somewhere – a long way from here?'

'Even then.'

'What makes you so sure?'

She indicated the deserted quarry behind them. 'You saw what happened as well as I did. Can't you guess what it meant?'

'It was creepy, if that's what you're getting at. All that green stuff sprouting out of his head!'

'I'm talking about what it told us.'

'It told me to get out of here!'

'No, more than that – it gave away their secret! The thing we've been trying to find out!'

'What kind of secret? The fact that there's some kind of plant inside their heads instead of a brain? How's that supposed to help us?'

'Because plants usually grow from seeds and it's the seeds that are important. They're the reason we've been cloned!'

Ross glanced back along the valley and then looked hard at Angie. 'So our doubles,' he said slowly, 'and all the rest of the clones, are just seed carriers? Is that it?'

'What are you going on about?' Nigel interrupted.

'It's the only explanation that I can see,' Angie said, ignoring Nigel completely. 'Hiding back there in the woods is something that's closer to plants than to animals. It all points that way – the unnatural summer growth, Tom's hatred of flesh, everything. Well, like all plants, that thing probably has seeds which need to be dispersed. And the method it's chosen is those clones. To such a creature they're nothing more than seed-dispersal units.'

153

Nigel sidled up beside Ross. 'She's crazy,' he whispered.

'No she's not,' Ross said, and pushed the younger boy away irritably. Bending down, he plucked a blade of grass growing from a crevice in the chalk and held it up. 'Even ordinary plants are clever in their own way,' he murmered. 'They use the wind, the birds, insects – oh, a hundred different methods of dispersing seeds.'

'So why should this thing be any different?' Angie cut in.

Ross nodded. 'D'you know something? I think we're onto it. Everything's beginning to fit together at last. Some plant-like creature lands here on earth. It's intelligent, but because it's a plant it can't move – it has to stay in one place. So what does it do? It makes use of the dominant species, the very species it's up against, to scatter its seed. And that species, as Nigel pointed out last night, is free to go anywhere.'

'Precisely. For all we know, those clones may be walking nurseries. They protect the seed until it's ready for planting, and then, when the time's ripe, they carry it well away from the parent plant. Nobody would dream of stopping them because they look as human as anybody else. And so the process goes on, from season to season, from country to country.'

'Which is why,' Ross added, 'there's no real escape for us. Not by running. Eventually they have to track us down.'

'Have you both gone crazy or something?' Nigel said. 'Tell them, Jack, tell them they're mad.'

But the old man's attention was fixed on the axe head. He worked the piece of flint backwards and forwards, wearing away the thin accumulation of rust and revealing the bright steel beneath.

'You understand what's going on, don't you, Jack?' Ross said, patting his shoulder encouragingly.

Without pausing in his self-appointed task, he muttered:

> *Here comes a chopper to chop off your head,*
> *Chop, chop, chop, chop.*

154

'I wish it was as easy as that,' Ross said sadly. 'Just a matter of chopping off their heads. But there are too many of them. And when it came to the point, none of us'd be capable of it anyway. They look too human.'

Jack glanced up, an angry gleam in his eyes. 'Not them, my lad. Not them babes in the wood, them puppets on his string. Only him, the dealer in meat, the green piper. He'll have no more green fingers when I've done.'

'You reckon that'll be enough, Jack?'

'He'll do for me.'

'And for me as well,' Angie agreed.

'But how will it help us?'

'It could finish the whole thing. This meat man of Jack's is the original music maker. The green piper. He's the intelligent one who's probably controlled everything that's gone on so far. Without him, the clones, including Tom, would be – well, what they are – mindless seed carriers. Directionless. He's the one who has to be stopped.'

Ross frowned. 'There's still the problem of finding him. Don't forget that.'

'We already know where he is. He's in the hollow. He has to be. That's where the music first came from. Where we found the scorch mark on the tree.'

As if to endorse her words, Jack whirled the axe about his head, the newly burnished steel glinting dangerously in the sunlight. 'I'm off,' he muttered, and began shuffling away.

'Hold on a second, Jack,' Ross called after him. 'What's the point of going there again? We've searched the hollow more than once. The last time we went I even ...'

He stopped abruptly and put both clenched fists to his forehead.

'What's the matter?' Angie asked.

'No, I *didn't*,' he said deliberately, speaking more to himself than to anyone else. 'I was just starting to when Tom arrived!'

Jack paused half way across the valley. 'You coming, Ross boy?'

'And it was dark,' Ross went on, 'the leaves so thick I couldn't see a thing!'

'Everyone's going crazy around here!' Nigel wailed.

Angie touched Ross's arm. 'What are you talking about?'

His hands fell slowly to his sides, and to her amazement he grinned at her.

'That's it!' he said. 'The thing that's worried me all along about the hollow!'

'What is?'

'That an elm tree's growing there! When virtually every other elm tree has been wiped out by disease.'

'Not the ones in Elm Walk,' Angie objected. 'They started to revive in the spring, remember?'

'Yes, but look at them. Still with lots of dead branches. Just a bit of young growth sprouting from the main limbs. But that one in the hollow . . .'

'. . . is as thick and lush as if it's never been sick,' Angie said quickly.

Again he grinned at her. 'I wonder why?' he said.

NINE

'I don't want to go down there,' Nigel complained.

Angie pulled him back into their hiding place amidst the dying fern.

'Hush,' she said, 'or you'll give us away.'

Jack, crouched near by, held up a warning hand and Angie also fell silent. There was a faint sound, as of someone moving slowly through the undergrowth, and Ross appeared over the lip of the hollow.

'As far as I can see there's no one about,' he whispered.

Angie frowned. 'That's not really a good sign, is it? If there was anything down there that needed protecting, someone would be on guard.'

'Possibly. Though we may have caught them unprepared.'

'I hope you're right.'

With Ross pushing Nigel before him, they crept from hiding and descended the slope into the hollow. The surrounding trees had dropped most of their leaves, their upper branches stark and bare. By contrast, the elm, dominating the lower part of the hollow, was still largely covered with foliage. Yet it too had begun to respond to the advancing season. Even now its yellowing leaves were drifting down on the light breeze; and in places it was possible to see through the thinning foliage to the lattice-work of branches within.

They stopped beneath the massive limbs and looked up. Shafts of mid-morning sunlight, tinted bright yellow by the fading leaves, illuminated what had once been the dark interior of the tree.

'Can you see anything?' Angie asked.

'Aye, there!' Jack growled, pointing one quivering finger upwards. 'There he is!'

Just visible near the top of the trunk was a long bulbous shape, dusky brown, almost merging into the sun-speckled background.

'Here, lend us your axe, Jack.'

The old man gave it up, not without some reluctance, and Ross swung himself onto the lowest limb and began climbing steadily.

'Take care,' Angie called anxiously.

His voice floated down to them, flat, disappointed. 'There's not much to be careful of. We're too late.'

They heard the sharp sound of an axe biting through dry wood, and something large but not particularly heavy came crashing through the branches. It landed with a hollow thud at their feet: a great pod-shaped object, well over two paces long and nearly as wide, but dried out and brittle. From its sides sprouted the remains of thick tendrils. It had no eyes nor ears. Only an oval mouth-like cavity; and near the top, a faded flower-shaped opening, revealing what had once been a seed-sack.

Ross dropped down beside them. 'It was a plant all right,' he said. 'A bit like one of those tropical gourd things you hear about. Its tendrils were buried in the trunk of the tree, like a parasite.'

Jack seemed to shudder slightly. 'He foxed me again,' he said tearfully, wiping a hand across his eyes. 'And me thinking I was bound to get him this time.'

Ross took the axe from his belt and proffered it to the old man. 'Here, do it anyway if it'll make you feel better.'

Jack raised the axe half-heartedly and let it fall onto the

swelling body of the pod. It caved in even under that feeble blow, revealing a womb-like interior. It was nearly empty, only three small bones nestling in the bottom. Ross picked them up and held them out to Jack.

'Take them,' he said, 'they're yours by rights.'

But the old man jerked his hand away hastily, letting them fall onto the leaf-strewn ground.

'Well that's that,' Ross said bitterly. He made as if to turn away.

'I don't think we've finished yet,' Angie said quietly.

He looked at her. She showed none of the disappointment he himself felt.

'What is there left to do?' he asked.

'There could be quite a lot.'

A flicker of hope appeared in Ross's eyes. 'What are you getting at?'

'Well last time we were here, Tom was standing guard over the hollow. Why isn't he here now? Or what's more to the point, why didn't he come to the quarry?'

'That was a bit odd,' Ross said with growing interest. 'As a seed carrier, you'd expect him to help the others. To go after his own double. I wonder why he didn't.'

'Maybe it's because the seed was implanted in him months ago,' Angie said meaningfully.

Ross took up the idea quickly. 'You mean the seed inside him is ripe?'

'More than that. It might have germinated. Taken root.'

Ross, his hand not quite steady, pointed at the shattered pod. 'In that case,' he said in an incredulous tone, 'he might even have turned into one of these things!'

She looked challengingly at him, Jack and Nigel momentarily forgotten. 'It's possible, isn't it?'

He nodded hesitantly, as if slowly coming to terms with the idea.

'There's just one problem,' Angie added. 'To change his form he'd need peace and quiet. He wouldn't want to risk being disturbed. So he's probably left this area. He could be almost anywhere.'

'Not necessarily,' Ross said, following a train of thought of his own. 'The pod was a kind of control centre – right? – telling the clones what to do. That's the way it looks to us anyway. Well who's controlling them now? If Tom really is turning into one of these pods, it must be him. I reckon he's still in these woods – hiding in some big tree – close enough to keep in contact.'

'But it's autumn,' Angie said, gazing up into the sun-streaked heart of the elm, 'most of the leaves have fallen. Even a big tree wouldn't give him cover for long.'

'There are evergreens,' Ross suggested.

'They're not usually thick and lush like an elm. He'd be too exposed.'

'What about a spruce? They're thick enough, with branches that go right down to the ground. A fully grown one would hide him easily.'

Angie glanced inquiringly at Jack. 'You know the woods best.'

But the old man was already chuckling quietly to himself. '*Oranges and lemons*,' he crowed delightedly, '*say the bells of St Clement's. You owe me ...*'

'Jack!' Ross interrupted, 'is there really a big spruce around here?'

'Aye, a big one,' he said slyly, winking at them. 'Big enough for the green piper himself.'

'Where?' Angie and Ross asked together.

'Up there on the ridge. About half way between here and the river.'

TEN

They could see the tree above them. It towered over its neighbours, dominating that part of the ridge. Amidst the fading colours of autumn it showed as a dense blue-green, like a tapering finger of shadow reared against the sky.

'Shall I scout ahead?' Ross asked.

'I'd rather you didn't,' Angie said uneasily. 'I have a funny feeling about this place. Better if we stick together.'

'Better for you, maybe,' Nigel muttered.

'That's enough from you, Shrimp. If you want to see that home of yours again, you'd better pull your weight for once.'

'I don't have to take orders . . .'

Before he could finish, Jack spun around and slapped him lightly across the mouth.

'Quiet!' he whispered hoarsely.

Except for one other occasion, earlier in the year, Ross had never seen Jack act aggressively. The sheer unexpectedness of it sobered them all and they fell silent.

'Ears like a hawk, he has,' Jack warned them. 'But we'll trim 'em for him this time.'

They ascended the hillside, picking their way between the trees. The damp undergrowth swished lightly against their legs, but otherwise they made no sound. All around them the woods were still, uncannily so, with not even a birdsong to disturb the

161

silence.

'What do you think?' Ross whispered, as they stopped about fifty paces below the ridge.

The whole of the tree was visible now, its lower branches resting on the ground like long trailing skirts. It was flanked by great banks of shimmering holly.

'I don't like the look of it,' Angie answered.

'D'you want to go back?'

'No, let's get it over with.'

They advanced slowly, Angie and Ross close together, with Jack to their right and Nigel dragging along behind. Only Jack appeared undaunted by the eery, strangely oppressive atmosphere, his old face fixed and intent.

'So far, so good,' Ross whispered.

But his very next step brought him to a sudden, jarring halt. Only a few paces from where he stood, lying half-buried in the faded ferns, was the body of Nigel's double. The exposed skin of its face and hands bore the unmistakable pallor of death; and the once-green tendrils sprouting from the head were now withered and discoloured, mere lifeless strings that drooped across the cheeks and hair.

'As you can see,' a voice said quite distinctly, 'we couldn't save him.'

They looked up, startled, as one of the lower branches of the spruce swung aside and two familiar figures emerged. They were, as Ross and Angie had realized all along, perfect replicas of themselves. Yet being confronted by their own faces, their own hands and arms and bodies, made them shrink back.

'Under the circumstances,' Ross's double went on evenly, 'you can hardly expect us to bid you welcome.'

Ross tried to answer, but failed. He took a deep breath to steady himself, and immediately felt Angie's hand tighten on his wrist.

'Look!' she whispered, too horrified even to turn away, 'look!' – pointing past the two figures, into the heart of the tree.

Despite the shadow cast by the overhanging branches, he could see clearly enough what had alarmed her. Pinned to the trunk of the tree by four curving green vines was what had once been Tom. The vines, each as thick as Ross's own arm, issued directly from the nose, mouth and ears, horribly distorting the face, making it barely recognizable. The head itself was bloated and enlarged, in the process of being torn slowly apart by the growing pod-like creature within; while from the neck down, the body had already begun to wither and putrefy, the once carefully pressed clothes hanging from now useless limbs. Only the eyes were still vaguely human: bloodshot and strained, they stared coldly, distantly, at the four unwelcome visitors.

'Oh my god!' Ross groaned.

He was shaking uncontrollably, he and Angie clinging to each other from shock. Behind them, Nigel, having sunk to the ground, seemed to be grovelling in the dry ferns.

Yet even this sight – his own body callously mutilated by the alien thing growing and burgeoning within it – was incapable of unsettling Jack.

'The green piper in person,' he said slowly, almost with relish, his voice steady, controlled, as though this were no more than he had envisaged. 'The meat man himself, waiting here for his old mate to come and find him – for the chopper man who's been listening to the bells and is ready to do his duty.'

'Your duty,' Angie's double corrected him ominously, 'was completed months ago.'

But Jack, surreptitiously tightening his grip on the axe, rambled on undaunted, 'Well here I am, yours truly, come to chop off a certain head like I'm told to in the story.' He chuckled mirthlessly and stroked his chin, his fingers rasping on the stubble. 'Oh not your story maybe, but one a bit like it. About paying debts: a head in exchange for a finger, for instance. That's fair, I reckon.'

He paused and smiled at the two pairs of expressionless eyes staring back at him.

'Your imbecile friend,' Ross's double said, 'has misunderstood the case altogether. All four of you have been permitted to approach this place for one purpose only. Not in order to seek vengeance, but merely to complete the cycle.'

Angie, not without visible effort, returned the blank incurious stare. 'What cycle?' she asked defiantly.

'Why, the cycle of regeneration. The transformation of flesh into vegetable life.'

'You mean we've been lured here to . . . to . . .?'

Her likeness nodded. 'Your death is both inevitable and necessary,' the cold voice informed her. 'You have been superseded. In addition, you must answer for this' – pointing to the dead body which lay stretched out in the grass.

'That was hardly our fault!' Angie protested.

'You must surely realize,' her double continued, ignoring her outburst, 'this is an unpardonable act. I do not speak of the destruction of the body, but of the precious green life cradled within it.'

'If you're talking about acts of destruction,' Angie replied hotly, 'then what about the deaths of all those children down there in the caves?'

Her own face, identical in every way except for the eyes, half turned away, as if in disdain. 'That was of little account to us. We have already told you, the destruction of flesh, of animal life, means nothing.'

'We'll see about that!' Ross muttered.

'Ah, I fear not.'

No observable signal was given. The tree above them merely seemed to shudder slightly; the bloodshot, horribly distended eyes of Tom rolled balefully in their direction. And all at once, accompanied by a rustling in the tall banks of holly, two groups of children stepped into the open, their faces completely impassive. Moving quickly, they fanned out into a half circle, cutting off any hope of retreat.

'Now what was it you intended?' Ross's double asked

164

pointedly.

Ross, conscious of his own helplessness, remained silent, looking with dismay at the harsh, unyielding faces on all sides and finally beyond them to the grotesque, putrefying body pinioned to the tree.

'In that case,' he was told, 'I think we may proceed.'

'What are you going to do?' Angie asked in a frightened voice.

'Exact justice. Beginning, as is fitting, with your young friend.'

Again there was no obvious signal, no actual word spoken. Tom's bulging eyes, all that remained of the once familiar face, swivelled meaningfully in their direction, and straight away ready hands reached out and took hold of Nigel, drawing him to his feet and forcing him backwards, away from the tree, out onto the sunlit hillside.

'Ross!' he squealed in panic, his narrow face distorted with terror. 'Stop them! You've got to stop them!'

Ross tried to break through the half circle, but he was met by an immovable wall of bodies, strong arms and hands thrusting him back into the tree's sombre shadow. He turned desperately towards Jack, with Nigel screaming shrilly in the background.

'Do something!' he pleaded. 'They're going to kill him!'

But to his amazement, Jack merely slumped to his knees, his face collapsing into a mask of fear. 'Spare me!' he blubbered. 'I'm just a useless old thing, that's all. Not a kid, like them.'

'Get up!' Ross roared at him. 'That won't do any good!'

He tried to haul Jack forcibly to his feet, Angie joining him, both of them tugging at his arms. But he cringed away from their touch, his face vacant with horror. They bent over him, pulling at his loose clothing – and that was when he whispered his message, the words so faint that they barely caught them: a short, urgent command meant for their ears alone.

There was a brief lull as they grasped fully what was expected

165

of them. Slowly, deliberately, they straightened up. Then, in unison, they turned and lunged desperately at their own doubles, while Jack leaped to his feet, the axe poised above his head.

The rest, for the two children, was largely lost in pain and confusion. Angie was met by an implacable vision of herself, steel-hard hands grasping her by the throat, the fingers tightening so convulsively that the sky quivered and darkened above her. Ross met a similar fate: a single stunning blow that crushed him to the ground. Through a blur of shadows he saw the tree tip sideways and threaten to fall on him. With an effort that wrenched him inside, he forced himself upright. But he could no longer see or hear clearly. There was a roaring inside his head; a sound of distant shouting; a face, eerily familiar, pressed close to his own; and a sense of being clawed at by unseen fingers. The shadows thickened, gyrating about him, a weight bearing down irresistibly upon his chest. And finally, all at once, silence.

He lay quietly, almost passive, listening, as his vision slowly cleared. Somewhere near by he could hear a wheezing and gasping; and a little further off, someone sobbing miserably. The weight was still there on his chest, but curiously inert. He sat up and the body of his double rolled off him. It was alive, breathing, warm to the touch, but with the intelligence, the directing consciousness, somehow absent, the eyes dulled over and unseeing. Ross looked about him in astonishment. All the other clones were in the same condition: lying exactly as they had fallen, their bodies still technically alive, but with the spark gone out of them. Their minds empty, barely existing, only the flesh remaining.

'What happened?' Angie asked in a croaky voice.

She was also sitting up, gingerly fingering her bruised throat.

They both looked across at the tree, to where Jack was doubled up, gasping for breath, struggling to recover. The axe was still held in his gnarled old hand, its burnished edge now stained with a greenish sap. Ross went over and put an arm around him.

'You did it, Jack!' he said admiringly, 'you did it!'

Beside them, no longer attached to the tree, lay the distorted remains of Tom, the four tendrils which had once preserved him now severed, cut off close to the face, their jagged ends dripping sap. Thankfully, the bloodshot, straining eyes had closed in death, robbing the ruined face of its last vestige of humanity.

Jack straightened up and wiped the sweat from his forehead. 'Old Jack was nimble that time,' he said huskily, 'and quick too.'

He tried to laugh, but broke into a fit of coughing.

'Steady, Jack,' Ross said, holding him – noticing with a mixture of concern and amazement how frail and thin he felt.

Angie crawled towards them, still with one hand to her bruised throat.

'What about Nigel?' she croaked out.

As if in response to her question, there was a movement amongst the bodies strewn across the sunlit hillside and Nigel stood up. His clothes were torn, his face and arms scratched, his glasses hanging from one ear.

'You all right, Shrimp?' Ross called.

Nigel, his thin body racked with sobs, straightened his glasses and glared accusingly at them through the one unshattered lens. 'They could have killed me for all you lot cared,' he said self-pityingly.

'If it hadn't been for Jack here,' Ross admonished him, 'they really would have finished you off.'

'D'you expect me to believe that? What could he do? He's mad, like everyone says.'

'Come on, Nigel,' Angie said coaxingly, 'calm down. It's all over now. You'll soon be able to go home.'

'Home? But ... but ...'

167

'There's nothing to stop you now, Nigel.'

He glanced around him at the fallen bodies, bewildered at first. Then, as the truth of her words gradually dawned on him, he backed slowly away, gathering confidence with each step.

'Hey, wait a minute!' Angie called, but he had already scurried off down the hillside.

'What d'you expect?' Ross said with disgust.

'I'm not sure we can really blame him this time,' Angie said. 'After all, there's nothing to keep any of us here now. I'll be glad enough to get clear of this place myself.'

She moved away from the tree, out into the pale sunlight, fully expecting Ross and Jack to follow. But they both hung back.

'Aren't you coming?' she asked.

Ross shuffled his feet uneasily. 'What are we going to do with these?' he said, indicating the fallen bodies.

She stayed where she was, unwilling to step back into the shadow of the tree. 'No one will find them up here,' she said. 'Can't we leave them where they are?'

He considered the question seriously. 'No, I don't think we can.'

She eyed the grisly remains of Tom distastefully. 'Why not? They're just empty bodies, with nothing inside them. Now that thing's destroyed' – pointing to the distorted face and shrivelled body – 'there's no mind, no intelligence, to direct or guide them.'

'I don't care,' Ross said doggedly, 'they still . . .' He struggled for the right words: '. . . they still look like real people – people I know. We can't abandon them here. That would make us as bad as the piper, treating them as so much useless meat.'

Angie hesitated and finally nodded in agreement. 'Yes, I see what you mean.'

She returned to the tree, stepping carefully between the silent bodies. 'Well?' she asked.

Ross scratched his head. 'Maybe . . .' he began helplessly.

But it was Jack who came to their rescue once again. 'Time we took a leaf out of the piper's book,' he advised them.

'How're we going to manage that?'

'Old Jack'll show you.'

He dropped the axe and began rummaging through Tom's clothes. 'Here's what we need,' he said, holding the pipes up for both of them to see.

Angie, impressed by the old man's reasoning, responded immediately. 'Marvellous,' she said admiringly. 'You're a clever man, Jack. Beating the piper at his own game.'

Ross was slightly more dubious. 'D'you reckon it'll work?'

'Stands to reason,' Jack said. 'Not for two of them – they'll have to be buried. But it'll do for the rest.'

He raised the pipes to his lips and blew. A thin wavering note issued out, reedy and uncertain. Yet it was all that was needed. Limbs began to twitch, hands to open and close, and one by one the fallen children rose slowly to their feet, their faces turned vacantly, robot-like, in the direction of the music.

'Where to, Jack?' Ross asked.

The old man took a deep breath. 'Where else?' he said.

And blowing wheezily on the pipes, he led the silent, staring throng over the ridge and down towards the river crossing.

PART IV

WINTER

'Well it's a mystery to me,' Mrs Bowles said, shaking her head first at the shopkeeper and then at Angie. 'Nearly two months now and not a sign of them. Vanished.'

Mr Hughes was standing with his large stomach pressed against the counter. 'Ah yes, a mystery right enough,' he assented. 'All those search parties scouring the countryside day after day; police turning the village upside down. Like everyone else, I thought something would come of it. But no, not a thing.'

'It's not a pleasant thought, I know,' Mrs Bowles said, 'but I doubt whether we'll ever hear word of them now. If you ask me,' she murmured darkly, 'it was a case of a kidnapping that went wrong.'

Mr Hughes nodded his head sadly. 'There're plenty of people in this area who'd agree with you. Even the police seem to have come round to that way of thinking.'

'Meanwhile,' Mrs Bowles sighed, 'all those poor mothers, just waiting. A terrible effect it must have had on them.'

'Not just on the mothers.' Mr Hughes leaned across the counter, addressing Mrs Bowles and Angie in a low confidential tone. 'Take old Jack, for instance. I had hopes, earlier in the year, that he'd come right. Almost the gentleman, he was. But since the tragedy – well, he's back to where he started.'

'Worse, if anything,' Mrs Bowles added.

'Personally,' Mr Hughes went on, 'I put it down to all that police questioning. I hear they held him at the station for days. Not that you can blame them: they had their job to do. But at the end of it all, there he was, back to his old self. Mad as a hatter!'

'Yes, a hopeless case,' Mrs Bowles replied sympathetically.

Encouraged by her attitude, the shopkeeper leaned even closer. 'Just between ourselves,' he murmured, 'and without wishing to be unkind, I can't help feeling sometimes that he would have been less of a loss than some of those dear children.'

Mrs Bowles nodded vigorously. 'Come to that,' she said, 'he isn't the only one we mightn't have missed.'

Angie, silent until then, stepped away from the counter. 'You can't really mean that!' she said hotly.

Mrs Bowles looked sternly at her daughter. 'You think I'm being malicious, my girl, but I'm not. I'm only referring to the injustice of it. To have some that I could mention still here when all those other poor children ...'

'But that's a horrible thing to say!' Angie insisted angrily. 'What have Ross and Jack ever done to you?'

'Don't you raise your voice to me!' Mrs Bowles replied sharply, 'Especially in connection with that young man. There was a time, back in the autumn, when I thought he might be changing his ways. He was really polite, respectful. What a boy of his age should be like. But of course it didn't last. Blood will out, as they say, and ...'

She was interrupted by the whir of the buzzer and Ross himself entered the shop. He was dressed in old clothes, his face and hands smeared with dirt.

'Speak of the devil!' Mr Hughes muttered.

'And the state of him!'

Ross ignored their remarks, looking straight at Angie. 'We're nearly done,' he said.

174

'The whole thing?' she asked.

'Just about. Jack's putting the finishing touches.'

'Then I'll come.' She walked resolutely across to the door.

'And where do you think you're off to, my girl?'

She looked back briefly. 'I need a change of air,' she said.

The door buzzer whirred and she and Ross emerged into the cold wintry lane. In the still, brittle atmosphere the bare trees seemed to reach up yearningly, craggy and black, towards the grey sky; and the children's breath billowed warmly about their faces, like thin smoke issuing from some hidden fire.

Angie made straight for the fence, but Ross called her back. 'Hold on, we have to fetch Nigel.'

'Does he need to come?'

'Jack says so. He thinks we should all be there, out of respect.'

He entered the nearest garden and knocked on the kitchen window. Nigel himself answered the door. Before he could draw back, Ross grabbed him by the jacket collar and marched him back down the path.

'Mum!' Nigel squealed, struggling feebly in Ross's grasp.

An upstairs window opened and a middle-aged woman peered down at them. 'What are you up to now, Ross Miller?'

'We're just taking Nigel for a walk,' he called back airily. And then, in a fierce whisper which rendered Nigel instantly docile, 'You'd better make this look convincing, Shrimp, or I'll brain you!'

With Angie's help, he bundled the younger boy over the fence and together they struck out across the field. Nigel, perhaps sensing the grim determination of his companions, made only one protest. 'What about my overcoat? I'll freeze!'

Ross took off his own thick woollen scarf and wound it roughly around Nigel's neck. 'Here,' he said, 'this'll have to do instead.'

From then on they said little, all three solemnly aware of the purpose of their journey, plodding silently through the bare

175

leafless wood. As if by mutual consent they skirted the hollow, unwilling to venture close to the two giant trees, and were soon descending the long winding path towards the river. At one point they had a clear view of the huge spruce that dominated the ridge to their right; but they glanced hurriedly away, not caring to think about the two leaf-strewn graves hidden beneath those spreading boughs – quickening their pace now they could detect the murmur of moving water.

The river was low and they had no difficulty in crossing the causeway. On the far side, the mouth of the cave – like a single dark eye set into the hillside – stared dully down at them. Ross and Angie had originally wanted to close up the entrance altogether, but Jack had persuaded them to leave it as it was, to avoid arousing suspicion in the village.

Now Angie paused and looked again at the dark opening. 'Do you really think we were right not to wall it up?' she asked doubtfully.

Ross shrugged. 'Probably. Once the search party had drawn a blank, I expect the police crossed the caves off their list.'

'We were just lucky they didn't find anything,' Nigel broke in, the memory of those anxious days making his voice tremble.

'I'm not sure it was luck,' Ross said. 'The police had no reason to believe the kids were in there in the first place. And anyway, it would've taken weeks, maybe months, to check all the tunnels. There're hundreds of them, some of them dropping straight down into deep water.'

'I never realized how far they stretch,' Angie added, 'until that day Jack led all those . . . those creatures inside. He was gone so long I thought he was never coming out. God knows where he took them.'

'That's one thing about Jack,' Ross said proudly, 'you can always rely on him to do the things that really count.'

Angie nodded, glancing enquiringly along the bank. 'Where is he now?'

'Up above, finishing the cairn.'

They scrambled up the steep hillside. Jack was waiting for them at the very top, sitting beside a rough pyramid of loose stones.

'That's the best I can do, Ross boy,' he said.

'It's fine, Jack.'

They grouped themselves around the cairn, standing with downcast eyes. After a few minutes of silence, Nigel began to fidget.

'Is this all we're going to do?' he asked, a note of petulance in his voice.

'What else is there to do?' Jack replied slowly. 'Memory's all we have to offer them now.'

'But shouldn't we have brought something? You usually put flowers on a grave.'

Jack, hat in hand, pursed his lips sceptically. 'After what's happened, lad, I don't think they'd thank us for flowers. Not more plants. Not for them.'

'Then what are we standing here for? What's the good of it? Or of this heap of stones? They're all dead, aren't they?'

'Watch it, Shrimp,' Ross growled.

But Jack shook his head sorrowfully. 'No, leave him be,' he said. 'We've done all we can for them, though it's little enough. You run off home now, Nigel lad.'

It was all the encouragement Nigel needed. After an I-told-you-so look at Ross, he slithered quickly down the hillside towards the river.

Left alone, the three friends continued to stand around the desolate heap of rocks. A thin, icy wind had risen and was gently stirring Jack's wispy hair.

'In a way he's right,' Angie said. 'We should have brought something.'

'Like what?' Ross asked.

'There's always this,' Jack said unexpectedly.

He rummaged in his overcoat pocket and produced the pipes once used by Tom. Placing them on the ground, he smashed them with his heel. Then, collecting the shattered pieces in both hands, he tossed them up into the breeze.

'Well that's the end of the piper,' Ross commented.

Jack seemed hardly to have heard him. 'For them,' he murmured, watching the straw-like fragments sail away in the wind, 'boys and girls all. For those sleeping here, and for all the others that have gone before.'

Angie looked at him doubtfully. 'What others, Jack?'

The watery-blue eyes gazed into space. 'Them that he took long ago.'

'But he only came here last spring.'

The old eyes swung round towards her. 'Did he?'

'Yes, you know he did.'

'Then how did he get to use the story of the pied piper?'

'He must have learned about it. It was something he copied, that was useful to him.'

'Let's hope so, lass.'

'What are you getting at, Jack?' Ross asked sharply.

Those old eyes, which he had always remembered as gentle and vague, were suddenly hard, unwavering. 'It could be that he invented the story himself, lad.'

Ross's face, reddened by the cold wind, turned abruptly pale. 'But it would mean he'd been here before! That there have been other invasions just like this one! That the story of Hamelin isn't just a . . . a story!'

'No, worse than that,' Angie put in quietly.

'Worse?'

'Yes, because there's the future to consider. If Jack's right, he or something like him could come again.'

Ross swung back to face the old man. 'The future, Jack! What'll we do?'

Jack shrugged, his wispy hair blowing wildly in the rising wind. 'As to that, lad, we're out of it now. We've done what we can, same as they did in Hamelin. The future'll have to take care of itself.'